SHIN YU PAI

ENSŌ

entre ríos books

ENTRE RÍOS BOOKS
www.entreriosbooks.com
Seattle, Washington

ENSŌ
Copyright ©2020 Shin Yu Pai

ISBN: 978-0-9973957-9-2

First Edition. ERB 013.
Printed in the United States.

Our books are proudly distributed by:
SMALL PRESS DISTRIBUTION
www.spdbooks.org
800.869.7553

DEVOTION

I roll the ball of golden wax
between my thumb and forefinger

leftovers gleaned from the gallery
floor, during the artist's installation

of giant cera alba ziggurats
shimmering pollen fields that

light up my imagination

the soft perfumed artifact
I take with me to tuck away

in the bottom drawer
of an unfinished cedar shrine

a keepsake activated &
sanctified so long ago,

this token
   I held back for myself

CONTENTS

PREFACE
MICHAEL LEONG

We often imagine poems as private expressions that begin in the mind and end on the page; though accurate for many cases, such a conception of poetry is necessarily restrictive. However one wants to categorize Shin Yu Pai's *Ensō* (a document of auto-curation that honors both product and process, a kind of creative nonfictional *Künstlerroman*, an illustrated *prosimetrum*), it is a model book—in its expansiveness of vision—to teach us how to extend poetry beyond the page as part of a publicly engaged, collaborative, and multimedial practice. I should hasten to add that although Pai, as a former poet laureate of the City of Redmond, is adept at bringing poetry into environments outside the dimensions of the printed codex through site-specific installations and video projections, anyone who is familiar with her writing knows that she frequently fuses design, layout, and versification in creating an imaginative *mise-en-page*.

She enjoys breaking free from the baseline of the justified left-hand margin to create a dynamic zone teeming with rich phrasings, expressive spacing, and surprising significations. In short, Pai excels both on and off the page as she carefully contemplates issues of language, form, and genre no matter the scope of the project.

Pai is a poet of discipline in the positive sense of being wholly dedicated to what she calls "the ongoingness of a regular practice." Her artisanal practices—rigorous acts of commitment, concentration, and devotion—have engaged with a variety of time frames, demonstrating an allegiance to the variegated times of meaningful activity in contradistinction to the standardized time that structures capitalist work. For example, she has written haiku every week for a year; ekphrastically documented the same space over the span of twenty years; stenciled apples in a public orchard to demonstrate the differential exposure to sunlight; and spent several months cutting windows into the covers of her book *Sightings* to reveal text printed on the title page.

Indeed, "practice" is an important word in describing Pai's artistic life; it, or its cognates, occur many times throughout the illuminating essays contained in this book: "I revisited practices, like Japanese tea and translation." And: "Haiku writing has brought forth a kind of communal writing and practice that has included everything." The word "everything" here is not merely gratuitous. Consider the following haiku that compresses within its diminutive structure a density of observation and feeling:

> just shy of thirty-five weeks,
> tsukimi chakai—I gaze
> at the ripening moon.

In presenting what T. S. Eliot might call an "objective correlative," Pai meaningfully juxtaposes ritual and gestational/reproductive temporalities while also connecting the micro- and macroscales of biology and astronomy. In the poem titled "Practice," she asks, "but isn't there / only this work? / day after day / heaps of words piling / up on my writing desk." A disciplined writer, who adventurously throws herself into her work, Pai is also a poet of many disciplines that go well beyond the boundaries of her writing desk. Open to an impressive range of artistic fields and methods, she is also a practitioner of book arts and photography. It is not surprising, then, that Pai has self-consciously put herself in a lineage of Asian and Asian American women artists who work in and across varied media—Noguchi Shohin, Ikka Nakashima, Yoko Ono, and Mei-mei Berssenbrugge, to name just a few. So too does Pai embrace the many cultural functions that poetry in its myriad material instantiations—from historically evocative visual poems executed through chlorophyll printing to a cloth broadside stitched with red thread to protest against a local hate crime—can perform for its communities. In other words, if Pai, as consummate craftswoman, proficiently works with the materiality of her media, she, as public poet, also considers the vital communal issues that matter.

Ultimately, *Ensō* celebrates a versatile sensibility that, to quote from Pai's title poem, "emerges [from] the place of possibility," that, however bound, is "upheld by [a] sense of boundlessness."

INTRODUCTION
SHIN YU PAI

Twenty years ago, I worked at the Dallas Museum of Art organizing the training of the museum's docents. The curator arranged a visit for us with Wolfgang Laib, the German artist who makes sculptures out of hand-harvested flower pollen, grains of rice, unending cartons of whole milk, and other natural materials.

The gallery welcomed us with the sweet smell of beeswax. Golden bricks of cera alba lay waiting to be added to the artist's monumental ziggurats. The brilliance of the yellow grains of pigment he sifted into tapestry-sized installations conjured up the edges of Rothko's color-field paintings. Moving through the beauty of Laib's minimalist rooms, my eyes were met with brass plates filled with rice grains, ethereal pollen mountains. My lactose intolerance generally repels me from dairy, but encountering Laib's shimmering *Milkstone* broke the conventions of my mind. A simple marble slab, supporting a suspension of pure white milk upon its surface, transformed into some other thing. When the artist spoke softly in measured response to the docents' questions about the places that informed his work, an idea of art-making that might be understood as an act of devotion began to emerge in me. Artful acts of offering.

I pocketed a fragrant ball of beeswax gathered from the "leftover" materials that didn't make it into a sculpture. This perfumed artifact I tucked away in the bottom drawer of my unfinished wooden shrine, alongside a small booklet with the name given to me by a Bhutanese rinpoche and the white scarf I received at the ceremony for my Buddhist refuge vows.

In 2018, I traveled to Bhutan as a fixer for Atlas Obscura and stopped at several sites of spiritual significance within the Buddhist lineage. I found myself thinking of Laib's work again. The places I visited were often found in nature, as in the case of Mebar Tsho, the Burning Lake the saint Pema Lingpa leapt into to recover sacred treasure. Or the long and winding path to Tiger's Nest Monastery, which is nestled in the mountains at over 10,000 feet. Along the paths to these sacred mountaintops, I came across thousands of tsa-tsa, tiny molded clay stupas, sacred art offerings left behind.

Nestled into cliff crevasses and cave niches were incense, rice, earthen relics finished in white, yellow, and other bright colors. In centuries-old temples, I felt my face flush with the heat of burning butter lamps. Everywhere I looked, golden bowls, filled with turmeric-stained liquid, and clear water—the humblest offering anyone can make.

Water is an offering that even the most poor can give. So is language. I regard poems as embodying a certain quality of grace. Vessels that reach beyond words to approach the ineffability of an offering, alchemized through the heart.

Practice is an aspiration—something that I attempt to realize from day to day. In this way, it's a vow that's meant to be renewed. It evolves, as we test out ideas on ourselves, and the consciousness expands to encompass more than we previously thought we knew about ourselves or the world.

As a project, *Ensō* traces the evolution of my creative practice and the many parts of the work that have helped to sustain an artful life. I was not attached to being a poet, but interested in using the instrument of language to make sense of the world. It has seemed fitting that this exploration should take more than one form, ever conscious of the presence and absence of language, the medium to which I feel most connected in spirit.

SIXTEEN PILLARS

As a newcomer to a city that I did not belong to, I asked myself what it would mean to engage with a single place over an extended period of time. How might that place become a part of my experience and live within my memory, just as I might become a part of its physical history and record.

THE SITE-SPECIFIC POEM

Known as simply Gallery 109, the dark room tucked away in a corner of the Art Institute of Chicago escapes the notice of most visitors. I began visiting the gallery in 1998, lured by Tadao Andō's elegant design for the space. Embedded in the Asian art galleries, amongst rooms of ceramic vessels and scrolls, the dimly lit room shows off the museum's Japanese antiquities. My nostalgia for a place that I'd never been to drew me into the space. My lover had moved to Kyoto to study tea, while I finished school. Bereft, I gazed at beautiful artifacts I imagined my beloved to be encountering in another place and time.

It gave me a strange comfort, reaching back to my earliest memories of visiting museums with my Taiwanese parents. Inevitably, we'd end up closely studying ink paintings of birds and flowers, or mountain landscapes—my father's favorite subjects. Even before my brother and I were born, my parents traveled long distances to experience Asian culture. As new immigrants living in rural Missouri, they drove 170 miles to visit the Chinese art collections of the Nelson-Atkins Museum, one of the few places where they could see their language and cultural symbols reflected back to them.

In Chicago, I hadn't yet discovered the rich genre of ekphrastic poetry, although like most college English majors, I'd spent time committing Keats's "Ode on a Grecian Urn" to memory. I studied the artworks displayed in the Andō gallery with care, noticing the visitors entering and filling the space around me. How they interacted with the silence, how they interacted with one another. The patient exchange between a father and his young daughter particularly struck me. And out of these observations sprang the first poem.

THE GATHERING
AT THE
ORCHID PAVILION

Entering a darkened room
to pass between sixteen pillars
of equal height and depth,
ten feet high and one foot square,

I place my hand against the grain
hold my ear to a column
listening for something
like the sound of trees.

Across the room
six folded screens
colored ink and gold on silk

the specks of turquoise in those mountains
glimmering points of light
from a distance
the shine of moss

in memory like the lights
of houses in the hillsides
lanterns in the sea
of winter nights.

Mist erases crags and peaks.

Bearded scholars on blankets
read to one another
calligraphing poems
under shade of bamboo and plum

as servants fill cups
with rice wine
floated downstream
on lotus pads.

My breath clouds the casing
as I think of humidity
and the desire to touch.

The door of the gallery opens.
A father and his daughter.

I think we've seen this one before, the girl says.
They look for the place where the story begins.
The girl kisses glass.

Where does the story begin?
father insists gently.

In the mountains, the girl cries.

Traces of handprints left on glass.

It starts here, she says.
Here.

I'd fallen in love during a year spent studying at Naropa, a small Buddhist college nestled in the foothills of the Rocky Mountains. In search of the local tea ceremony teacher, I went to the campus teahouse to find the sensei. She remained elusive, but he was always there—opening the door, cleaning the tatami mats, preparing for tea. We regarded each other from a safe distance. I started coming around for lessons, and shyly acquiesced to preparing tea when the teacher asked. In the tiny kitchen at the back of the teahouse, I spilled bright green tea powder all over the mat, while anxiously trying to neatly scoop the tea powder into the natsume. His eyes were full of kindness, as he spoke softly to me, and took the tools from my hands to quickly mound a perfect mountain of matcha. His name was Bergman, or what translated as "Man of the Mountain."

In Colorado, I worked on a short collection of Chinese poetry with my father, who gave me a crash course in the classical poetic tradition. In my background readings, I discovered scholars—poets like Li Bai and Tu Fu—men of leisure who drank together and inspired one another's poems. I saw how the images from the painted screen on display in the Andō gallery mirrored this literary history.

Those years that I spent living in Chicago, I returned to the Andō gallery over and over again, with the idea that the experience of the space itself could be as profound as seeing its relics revealed. While the art might not rotate for long periods of time, the space of the gallery remained dynamic and ever changing in its continual influx of visitors who lingered beyond the typical speed-viewing of the modern, ten-second attention span. Stopping in the gallery became a part of my routine. As I began to shape a more artful life centered upon creative thinking and production, I revisited practices, like Japanese tea and translation, that had been significant to me in the past.

Tokyo Rose, the purveyor of Toguri Mercantile, a seller of Japanese sweets on Belmont Avenue, pointed me towards a tea teacher on the north side of Chicago. By the time I met Ikka Nakashima, she was already in her seventies. I didn't know until coming across her obituary recently that Sensei had been the second woman to receive the Order of the Rising Sun—awarded to those who

▲ Ikka Nakashima

My teacher, on Carmen Street, in the West Argyle neighborhood, north Chicago, 2003.

have made distinguished achievements in the promotion of Japanese culture. But what really added to Sensei's lore was her connection to a Tibetan lama in Boulder. He had paid her a visit in the hopes of persuading her to move to his mountain town to teach at the experimental college where I would eventually find myself.

I became Nakashima Sensei's student in Chicago, and after nearly a year of practicing with her, I received formal permission from her to undertake study. From Sensei, I learned the nuances of positioning the hearth in winter nearer to the guests. When to use a lighter-colored, wider bowl in summer, in order to evoke the coolness of ice. The shallowness of the drinking vessel that allows the tea to cool more quickly. I learned a new version of a tale that I had once come across while translating poems from the ancient Chinese—the story of the cowherd and weaving girl. Two star-crossed sweethearts, separated by the Milky Way, reunite by a bridge of magpies that forms on the seventh day of the seventh month, or tanabata matsuri. In the month of July, Sensei hung a scroll with poems inspired by the stars in the tokonoma and brought out a special cha-ire—a tea container viewed just once a year.

Sensei gave me the gift of permission to encourage my tea practice and to open a door to studying at the Urasenke school in Kyoto, where I could rekindle a romance with my lost love.

STILLNESS

columns you pass between
      tower high as bamboo stalks
         grouped in a grove

a white-haired guide
      prompts school students,
         to exit in silence
           now

this rawness in the back of the throat
      heart leaping forward

while the mind turns back

to the cool darkness of
      a tea teacher's home
         on West Carmen Street

      Monday nights
gakusei wore woolen
      sweaters, stockings
         under ankle-length
      skirts gathered neatly
under knees

      we knelt in practice
hot water, matcha warming a bowl

the chill of the gallery dissipating

My visits to the gallery ended when I left Chicago in 2000. The man I loved returned home and presented me with an ultimatum to begin a life together in a foreign city. I boxed up my books, sold my furniture, and moved south. Dallas, Texas, hadn't been my first choice. Living in the South for the first time, I felt acutely aware of cultural differences and expectations of gender. My eventual in-laws affectionately referred to me as "Daughter-in-Law Number One," not fully understanding the reverberations of such an "honorific." While I worked at a fine arts museum located across the street from a private collection of Asian artifacts, it was Andō's space that remained in my imagination.

I had entered into a world that belonged to someone else. The history of his childhood memories were written throughout the artworks housed in the museums that we frequented in Dallas and Fort Worth. Andō's gallery, by contrast, belonged to me alone. I had spent days, weeks, and months in the space watching life unfold and looking for something to be revealed to me about the rhythms of human life. Observed how bodies in a gallery mirrored the changing seasons, and surroundings, illuminating the analogy between Japanese time and the human experience. People became the art, as their personhood was magnified by the contrast with minimalism and silence of the space.

I saw that the visitors could reflect something of the changing seasons and sensibilities in their heavy, fur-collared winter coats and gloves, school jerseys, and ball caps with political slogans, in the same way that the curated displays of paintings revealed something about timelessness.

It seemed to me that the tracking of activity in Andō's gallery could mimic a quality of Japanese poetics—an attention to the passage of seasons and the feel of a specific place at a given time. I decided then that with every opportunity to return to Chicago, I'd revisit the Andō gallery and write a poem—new iterations of "The Gathering at the Orchid Pavilion."

SITE
SPECIFIC

a crop of new students
fresh-faced from St. Bridget's
Catholic converge upon
the gallery, names emblazoned

across the backs of royal blue
fleece sweatshirts: Aguilar,
Pacheco & Guernsey

girls in maroon polos &
dark skirts, shade of "old
Bordeaux" the rusted
patina of urban overpass

a boy named Isabella
races to claim the headset
first, a flat-screen station
now animating the room

loops footage from a ritual
concert: kuniburi no utamai—
narrative tunes reaching back
to the 10th century

facing the wall, he turns
his back to handcrafted
bamboo pipes while another
youth snaps a photo of

the stringed zither inlaid
with ceramic hand picks;
this kid sealed off by earbuds
no different than I, the poet

nose stuck deep inside
a notebook, attuned to
the private experience of
encountering the music within

giant stoneware pots
that never rotate off display
sing quietly of wind

It was several years before I would return again. Much and nothing had changed. The ancient jomon jars placed along the perimeter of the room remained where they had always been. In an effort to embrace technology, the museum installed a flat-screen television with headphones that ran on a continual loop.

We continued to evolve as a couple. Our lives shifted as we tested new geographies together. We moved west and back south again. Embarked shyly and unsuccessfully on starting a family, while settling into a prosaic form of domesticity brought on by marriage.

Ten years later, the glass doors that sealed off the room from the rest of the Japanese collections were permanently removed. The Art Institute went high tech, projecting video and light upon the walls. Instead of antiquities filling the cases, modern Japanese fashion design dominated the displays. The quiet contemplative nature of the room shifted towards a different approach to engagement. The museum commissioned contemporary artist Jan Tichy to make a new work responding to the physical space. Beams of light bounced across the gallery, drawing the eye away from inward reflection.

Flooded by visitors intent on documenting intricate postures with their cell phone cameras, the integrity of the space was severely compromised by the Institute's desire to bring more people into the space. The essential quality of the experience was abandoned—namely one of mindful awareness, a keen observation elicited by the gallery's original quality of light.

I wanted to return to the origin, a time before poetry emerged in me, to recover a deeper calling to beauty.

BOLT

jomon jars replaced by plastic
mannequins, desiring definition
vacant body forms, scaffolding

to bear the float of haute
couture, Japanese fashion
Rei Kawakubo's slip:

"lumps & bumps"—a garment
of transposable parts, butt pads
shift to chest or hips

bee-stung knees, or a weight-
lifter's sinewy back; shoulders
like Tilda Swinton

the site-specific video install
lights up Andō's beams like
a fashion expo, visitors

careen down a catwalk
of columns, the space between
pillars, a stage for selfies

in silhouette, geometric slants
echo frames of denuded
posts, a scroll of light

unfurled against a wall
the artist's projection
measured patterns

of movable parts

I returned to the Andō gallery in 2016, nearly twenty years after my first visit. I'd become a mother. Taken long breaks from art-making and left parts of myself behind to shape a new identity and life.

The same decorative folding screen that was on view when I first began writing about the Andō gallery had come back on display.

I read the didactic label closely this time. It described a painting on the backside of the screen. Locked behind glass, this painting remained unviewable. In my imagination, I walked around the partition to close the circle and look upon an image of geese and reeds.

Curated alongside the image of leisurely literati stood a separate series of panels highlighting historical Japanese poets. As I scanned the portraits for names and faces that I might recognize, I realized how little had changed throughout the ages and cultures. Male poets outnumbered the women. One woman, completely concealed by her hair, might well have been anonymous. The didactic label was unsatisfactory, and had in fact always been lacking. The poems that I'd written back then and now were my way of disrupting the silence of these informational time capsules put forth by art curators. The poems were my effort to open up a space and time beyond what the label prescribed, to create something distinct from what was visibly enshrined, translating the other into a language of self. Finding beauty in absence, coming home to both longing and belonging.

REPRODUCTION

in the painted screen a woman
confined to a wheelchair sees
turquoise rocks pure as sea stacks
straight from the Pacific Northwest

fanned out at eye level, the image
on the reverse side pictures
Geese Among Reeds—a painting
I gaze upon in my mind's eye

recalling eighteen years ago
a first encounter with this partition—
the depiction of men at leisure,
overlooking somehow

a spring purification rite made
more real this day by the occasion
of my return to the windy city
for a friend's second marriage

I visit artworks in museums
like favorite family members
finding comfort in the fact
that nothing's changed after

major expansion, the gallery
restored to a simple display—
same panel, the unevolved language
I lifted for a poem; in the wings,

a six-panel screen beneath
dimmed lights lights up twelve
immortals with their poems,
five women in multihued kimono

portrayed alongside seven male
counterparts, the curatorial text
indicates no names, scribbled waka
verse hovering above each picture,

in one portrait, a poet's kimono
pools around her floating body;
in another, a woman's features
concealed by a dark curtain

of hair; in the third sketch
a female figure faces away from
the artist's gaze, I guess
at who they are—Izumi Shikibu

Sei Shonagon, Ono no Komachi
the only names I know, scan
across the screen to notice
each male bard meeting the eye

of his onlooker, angled at 45 degrees,
the faceless immortal the viewer
projects traits upon, a name
to claim a lasting place

gilded and burnished in gold
this screen made for "women's quarters"
dominated by virile likenesses,
I reach towards my own life,

in lieu of the art historical,
the imagination recomposes
the scene, I enter the divider,
to embody the faceless courtesan,

& in the final intervention
I displace the patriarchal form
enshrouded in mondokoro
to even up the numbers,

take my seat with symbols
of my own making: sixteen
stanzas for sixteen pillars
in this gathering space.

HAIKU
PRESENT

Tied together by friendship, it was a personal
and quiet book of daily observations and human
connection. A reflection of how we can support
and care for one another in the ongoingness of
a regular practice, stripped down to its essentials.

THE GIFT ECONOMY

My sensibilities of language have been informed by growing up with Taiwanese and Mandarin in my ear, and a strain of English that wasn't metrical. As a result, I've steered clear of form—in the same way that I approach prose with caution. Some poets revel in the turn of a sonnet and the crafted language of inherited forms, but for me, the shape of a poem arises out of studying the environment. That said, it can be useful for a writer to have a structure to work within, and my go-to form has always been haiku.

The compression of words and sentiment into a few imagistic lines form the basis of my approach to an observational poetics. Occasionally poems flow from the present moment. Those tend to be loosely grounded in an appreciation for Beat poets like Jack Kerouac, who experimented with Japanese verse. In what might seem a strange cultural exchange, it was through my exposure to the Beats—so wild and different than my life as a teenager in Riverside, California—that I began my own study of Asian literary classics and forms. It was through these uniquely American voices that I found there could be something to recover in the cultural origins that I turned away from.

The concision of the haiku creates a stripped-down quality—a leanness that leaves no room for fattiness or commentary. As a result, the inward eye must be diamond sharp, perfectly attuned to the interior space that informs observation. The images emerge effortlessly because they are the act of seeing, before the mind catches itself. I kept my love for haiku concealed from "real" poets, until meeting the filmmaker Tom Gilroy at the MacDowell Colony. I found a screenplay and a copy of Tom's book *The Haiku Year* tucked in my mailbox one morning. Written by an intimate group of friends, *The Haiku Year* fulfilled a promise. Everyone involved wrote a daily haiku for an entire year, trading these poems through the mail. It was a personal and quiet book of daily observations—included were facsimiles of the scraps of paper, old ticket stubs, and recycled product packaging on which poems had been hastily scribbled. It spoke to me as a way to support someone in the ongoingness of a regular practice, stripped down to its barest essentials. The poems I was writing at my residency were deeply engaged in the processes of visual art-making and the abstract imagination. The reappearance of haiku as a grounding force helped bring me back to the present. After years of working alone, it was a form that awakened new forms of poetic conversation.

One restless afternoon I hit a rut in my work; I took a drive with Tom and two other artists to a used bookstore in Dublin, New Hampshire. The New England countryside was shrouded in fog and the roads were covered in snow. Tom noticed me white-knuckle gripping the arm of the door and slowed the ancient Jeep. We arrived at the bookstore and scoured the shelves for hardcover books and secondhand poetry. Tom's enviable find that day near the checkout counter was a vintage series of stereoscopic photographs of old Japan— images in duplicate of kimono-clad geishas and Mt. Fuji in the distance. I collected vintage artifacts and books related to East Asia and tried my best to not begrudge his luck.

I shared some poems that I was working on with Tom and in response he gave me a copy of his haiku manuscript *Volunteer Geraniums*. The pile of papers were filled with short, urban poems animated by lines about cats, cherry blossoms, and everyday encounters. I typed up Tom's poems on my ancient Underwood, trimmed the sheets into a small chapbook, and hand-stitched the book together with red cord. On the cover, I stamped the word HAIKU and gave it to my friend the night before he departed.

After finishing my residency and returning to Boston, I came home to find a handful of postcards and envelopes from Tom filled with haiku scrawled on random scraps of paper waiting for me. On one of the stereographs, Tom had written:

> morning dove coos
>
> drowned out
>
> by jackhammers

The image, the one that I had coveted most, was a beautiful young girl in a golden yellow dress.

I remembered the seemingly simplistic form of haiku from my elementary school days. But what was missing in that early introduction was the complexity of specific rules that can inform the poet's use of seasonally specific language. Also absent was an understanding of the communal quality of the form through the practice of renga—how poets would gather for grand celebrations or on outings to swap, link, respond, and challenge one another with their verses. Back then I found myself on the fringes of a very masculine literary community. Poets gathered at Bill Corbett's house in the South End to watch Sunday football and carouse. I was one of a few young women in my circle, and a running joke was that the men in the group shared the other female poet amongst them. Collaborative exchanges emerged among my peers, but I felt more at ease turning towards the quiet, long-distance practice of being a poetic pen pal.

I wrote a haiku every week in 2015. A new group of friends took up the haiku writing challenge together, including a doctor, an activist, and several artists. I collected and shared the poems back to the group over email once a week, sometimes waiting to post my own until scanning the themes that people were working with, reacting to the weekly dispatches. Occasionally, I'd add lines to existing verses, transforming someone else's stanzas into linked verses.

In the end, we had a chronological archive of a year's worth of intimate reflection encompassing birth, death, work, life,

and love. We decided to call that collection *Haiku Not Bombs* after
a line in a sequence of linked haiku inspired by a newspaper story
of how the government of Thailand responded to civil unrest and
the threat of war among its provinces.

> over Narathiwat, Thailand
> one hundred million
> paper cranes

> missives of peace—
> war is over
> if you believe

> haiku
> not bombs
> origami art of war

We published *Haiku Not Bombs* as Collectivo Haiku with Booklyn
Artists Alliance in 2008 and celebrated with a reading in the East
Village. I flew out from Seattle for the event and finally met sev-
eral of the poets I'd been writing with for a full year. Then we
disbanded, off to pursue other projects. I missed the daily conver-
sational quality of our poems, the playfulness of looking carefully
at one's own mind and witnessing others in that same act, without
judgment. Once in a while, I'd send a haiku postcard to Tom and
find an envelope in my mailbox with poems scrawled on napkins.

Four years later, we brought a smaller collective together to produce
collection of poems to benefit Tom's town library in Rensselaerville,
New York. Over a month, we wrote poems in small, spiral-bound
notebooks made with checkout cards repurposed from library
books. Looking back, I can see that a few themes emerged as we
wrote together—aging, eros, politics, and reflections on gender.
How our personal expressions found new meanings and resonance

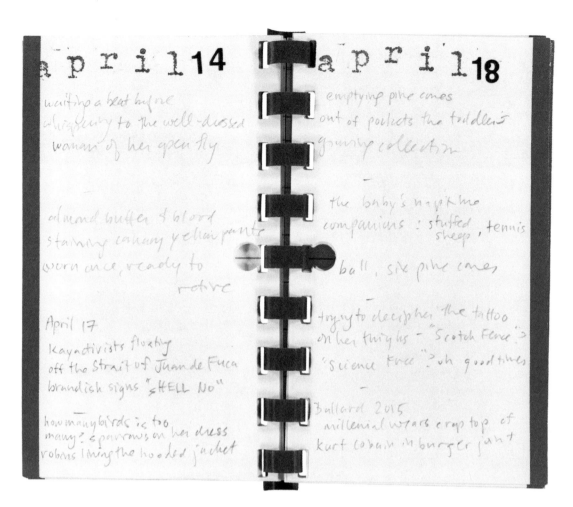

**▲ Rensselaerville
Festival of Writers
Haiku Project**

Working notebook with
daily entries, 2013.

in this community of practitioners. The originals were collected and auctioned for the library fund. The musician in the collective, Michael Stipe, surprised us all by recording his favorite poems from the project in a reading that was unrehearsed and spontaneous.

When I started writing haiku, decades ago, I saw it as an easy form, something accessible to young writers. And it can be that, something readily learned. But as my practice has deepened, and I uncovered its roots in communal writing, it's become a form that sustains me. One that I can imbue with anything and everything. A creative form, that's adapted to me—informing the way-finding texts that I wrote for public bike trails in Redmond and the poetic texts that I've printed on glow-in-the-dark balloons for children. These poems are small but powerful gifts, everyday jewels that brightened my daily work in the early days of motherhood when I did not have the energy or mind to shape longer poems, and in times when the concision of short verses has been precisely necessary.

F.O.W. HAIKU PROJECT 2013

F.O.W. HAIKU PROJECT

2013

game show's lone female
hopeful buzzes in the answer first:
what is the glass ceiling?

Shin Yu Pai

the season's new blooms
bring a tear to my eye
"what's the pollen count?"

Patrick So

bill o'reilly explodes at laura ingraham
because we need a headline
that will make you click through.

Michael Stipe

sunny side of 4th Ave
the difference between
winter and spring

Jim McKay

catching myself ignoring
the tabletop blossoms -
the cafe hired a new waitress

Tom Gilroy

bra shopping deterred
by the anarchists gathering
Occupy Westlake Park

Shin Yu Pai

**RENSSELAERVILLE
FESTIVAL OF WRITERS
HAIKU PROJECT**

REGRET SHARP USELESS
A NEGATIVE REMINDER
OF BEING ALIVE

SHELLY SILVER

FOUNTAIN, JET NOISE, BIRDS,
DOGS, TRAFFIC, SIREN, KIDS, FRIDGE
WHO'S THE COMPOSER?

STEVE PETERS

CELL RING WAKES ME;
EMAIL PIC,
THE LUNAR ECLIPSE

TOM GILROY

FIRST APPLIANCE PAID
FOR WITH POEMS --THE CHILL SETS IN--
ONE FRIDGE PER DECADE

LISA GILL

IN THE ALLEY, THE KENYAN LABORER
PICKS UP USED NEEDLES W/ GLOVED HANDS -
WHAT KIND OF ASYLUM IS THIS?

SHIN YU PAI

**Rensselaerville
Festival of Writers
Haiku Project**

◄ Letterpress cover and
haiku on cards, 2013.

▲ *Dish Towel Haiku*, 2014.

UNCOLLECTED HAIKU
2005–2019

THE EKPHRASTIC IMPULSE

Art and poetry inspire interrogations of both aesthetic and human experience. In this way, they converse intimately with one another in the kinship of parallel process.

THE ARTFUL EYE

The biggest influence on my poetic sensibility is not the work of another writer, but rather the exposure to the arts that I had as the child of an immigrant who also happened to be a creative virtuoso. My mother, Noko Pai, studied painting and fine arts and worked as a graphic designer in Taipei, before moving to this country. When she arrived in her late twenties, she spoke very little English. Despite becoming a mother to two children, the pull to hang on to her culture and language of origin surpassed the desire to master a new language. It didn't help that my father took a very exacting and perfectionist approach to correcting her English, crushing any curiosity to go further.

Everything she wanted to express was there in her paintings anyway, the objects she carved and shaped. She had her own language as an artist—her color palette, the range of materials she'd use to express an idea, and the human figures that filled her canvases, making our lives and imaginations in suburban Riverside a little less lonely. My mother moved between art-making practices seamlessly; she taught herself how to throw on a wheel and work with clay. When I was young, she cut and bound together small books in which I practiced my penmanship and experimented with drawing simple cartoons. She made amazing meals, replicating restaurant dishes, and grew, harvested, and processed much of our own food. The walls of our house evolved into a gallery of her ever-changing interests—images of beauty created to offset the poverty and ordinariness of our daily reality. She created a language that I wanted to know and enter into.

SIX PERSIMMONS

for Noko

after ruining another season's harvest—
overbaked in the kitchen oven then
rehydrated in her home sauna
Aunt Yuki calls upon her sister,

paper sacks stuffed full of orange
fruit, twig and stalk still intact
knows that my mother sprouts seedlings
from cast-off avocado stones, revives

dead succulents, coaxes blooms out of orchids
a woman who has never spent a second
of her being on the World Wide Web,
passes her days painting the diversity of

marshland, woodland & shoreline;
building her own dehydrator fashioned from
my father's work ladders, joined together
by discarded swimming pool pole perched

high to discourage the neighbor's cats
that invade the yard scavenging for koi
Vitamin D, she says, as she harnesses
the sun, in the backyard the drying device

mutates into painting, slow-dripped
sugar spilling out of one kaki fruit
empty space where my father untethers
another persimmon, he swallows whole

▲ Noko Pai

The artist in her studio,
Taiwan National Arts
Academy, Taipei, 1966.

The distance between my mother and me pointed me towards poetry, as a kind of idealized space where I could find a common language with her, through exploring her creative vocabulary and gestures. This may have led me to first write about the visual arts. The poems were conversation not just with artists but with the artworks themselves about the artfulness of art, and therefore the artfulness of life.

Beneath that layer of dialogue, I also felt a certain kind of creative selfhood in engaging with forms flexible enough to encompass multiple identities. I composed poems that took their cues from visual not literary culture. Hid myself behind the surfaces of these early poems, convinced that in those early days of coming into my identity as an Asian American writer that taking a position or expressing a perspective about my experience could not possibly serve me. Instead, I focused on hybridity, parallels between processes, and the ways of seeing that are unique to visual and poetic practice. This dissociation was an inherited approach. When it came to having earnest conversations with my mother about creative decision-making, we could never get far, in any language.

My work evolved beyond the trope of surfaces when I began to apply an anthropological perspective to thinking about the arts, to rethink how aspects of culture can be visually expressed and how images can be understood as artifacts of culture. Encountering writers working within the genre of documentary poetics, like C. D. Wright and Kaia Sand, helped me understand how socially engaged commitment can be deeply intertwined with one's poetic language.

I have never tired of responding to the visual arts through poetry, but my interrogations now reach past an image to approach a third kind of conversation that I'm interested in having—one that goes beyond artwork and maker to include the larger dialogue with the social circumstances under which a work of art exists.

MÉTAPHYSIQUE D'EPHEMERA

AFTER JOSEPH CORNELL

a pantry   *ceci*
ballet for   ÉCHAPPÉ
Jacques   EN RELÈVE   *n'est pas*
Offenbach   SOUS-SUS
                   ALLONGÉ   *une*
                   MENU TENDU
                   SAUTÉ   *écrevisse*

        demitasse   tossed
         caviar   salad
        absinthe   *à la*
        bouillon   *russe*
         silver
         spoon
       washboard
        & jug

POEM

FOR WOLFGANG LAIB

a life
of collecting pollen
from hazelnut bushes
a life of gathering word-grains
to find all you have wanted
all you have waited to say

five
mountains
we cannot climb
hill we cannot touch
perhaps we are only here
to say house, bridge, or gate

a passage
to somewhere else
yellow molecules
spooned and sifted
from a jar filled with

sunlight
           pouring
milk
       over
               stone

you are the energy
that breaks form
building wax houses
pressed from combs

a wax room
set upon a mountain
an offering of rice
nowhere everywhere
the songs of Shams

FEEDBACK

AFTER JOHN POMARA

the   push and   p u l   l
     of paint   sliding across a surface
rolling tremolo machine
paint flows off
the hard edge of aluminum
     Rorschach drips
read on the horizontal:

a   graph   body's
           of the   progress
stut-ter-ing
on the vertical—
a
screen-
play
glitches
on
8 mm
race
across
a
filmstrip
shifting

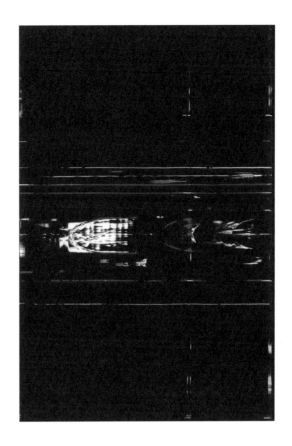

cut up

xerox

magnified

blow up

d r a g g e d across an electric eye

emanations of light from behind the screen

the absence of painter

presence of machine

the television a template

for a sketch enacted

in childhood

boxes full of light

reaching through the screen

the human hand

leaves its traces

DE STIJL

blocks of color
move across canvas
syncopated
                revisionist
divisionism—
a method of placing blue
        alongside yellow
to signify green
Seurat's influence
in Mondrian's early work:
the windmill at Blaricum
Dutch landscape painting
and years spent rendering chrysanthemums
collecting
images from nature
a subsequent progression
from reality to abstraction
rectangular planes
and the repetition of elements
red
blue
white
yellow
black
~~lines drawn, crossed out,~~
~~and drawn again~~
lines drawn, crossed out
 and drawn again
        to add more
boogie
woogie
dissonant
                harmony
measures of blue
        on the downbeat

SHIN YU PAI

De Stijl

▲ *De Stijl*
Pamphlet produced by
Christopher Rizzo of
Anchorite Press, Boston,
Massachusetts, 2004.

TENDING,
(BLUE)

contemplating
urban building creep,
two art fanatics launch

a scarlet red sphere
skywards at the exact
location of the future

Museum Tower, an empty
concrete lot, to test a theory
of infringement upon

an artist's field of vision

three years later
the glass skin
of the neighboring

luxury condo project
scorches the Nasher lawn
with too much reflected

light, the frame's
edges scaffolding
construction hoists

LIGHT REIGN

inside the sky—

viewing chamber

galaxy black

granite flecked

flooring reverses

a cutout of azure

light in the late winter

each echoing nightfall

stone mirror-map of

infinite constellation

s t a r   s h (r) i n e

altar   /   alter   /   alma

mater / matter / mutter moonward /

murmur   /   muster   /   muscle

muse   /   mute

POEM FOR
ART HANDLERS

Start from square one:
21 isometric cubes of varying sizes
with color ink washes superimposed
guidelines for a wall drawing,
a written instruction, intangible
scribbled notes and diagrams

find creative storage solutions—
three thousand pounds of Belgian
candies imported for a Gonzales-Torres
exhibition to be stored on the delivery
dock or held in low humidity
alongside Cannaletto?

if only we hadn't sprayed the crickets
raining from the ceilings, clogging
the elevator shafts, one step up
on the evolutionary food chain above
wingless insects feeding on the pollen
fields, engorged bugs leaving their tracks

wire a phone jack in the east gallery
and wait for Yoko Ono to call
she will telephone and tell you
to imagine a happening where
you clock out early after
letting loose at closing

a herd of starving cats
converging to lap up milk
pooling on the marble stone

MILKSTONE

the splash and spread
of milk poured over stone,
like paint applied to wet
watercolor paper
the slow bleed to edge
milk on Macedonian marble
tension of liquid on solid
surface
purer than pigment
laid over unprimed
canvas by Robert Ryman
caked with paint,
white on white,
a circle of milk poured
and pulled into a square
finger drawn milk
mandala
to flood the gates
turn a finger inwards
throwing a glance
the Buddha lifted a finger
in a crowd of thousands
gesture
overflowing
fullness
liquid trails gliding
into seamless, trembling
being

MAKING BOOKS

At its most basic level, making a book by hand is
a method of controlling the means of one's own
creative production. The organization of language,
structure, and the reading experience are directly
shaped by decisions that go beyond the breaking
of a line or the placement of words across the page.

STRUCTURES OF THOUGHT

When a box of my book *Sightings* arrived, I took an X-ACTO knife to the covers and hand-cut rectangular holes out of all 750 books. The poet Brenda Iijima had described to me the act of sandpapering her book covers and distressing them in a clothes dryer to age them—to apply the hand of the artist and make the books a little less mass-produced, a little less shiny. While I'd worked on design details with book artists for smaller editions, I hadn't thought that this kind of tampering was possible with a book designed for trade.

I'd approached San Antonio designer Rolando Murillo to design *Sightings* after seeing his work on Anthony Flores's *Hold Your Tongue, Poet*—an exquisite, pocket-sized, staple-bound chapbook that made me reconsider the artfulness of the self-produced book. Flores's book succeeded in being typographically elegant, spacious despite its scale, and deliberate in its visual imagery, which evoked medical and natural illustration alongside surrealist symbolism and street art. I'd learned the value of having a first-class designer from working with J. B. Bryan on my first full-length book, *Equivalence*. J. B.'s grounding as a painter and the fineness of his eye made all the difference in the feel of the books that he produced for La Alameda Press and for others.

Rolando and I discussed a physical intervention that could be performed on the book and settled upon windows cut into the cover and handstamped interiors. It took many months, one handmade cardboard guide, two dozen blades, and one ink pad. I found the repetitiveness and exacting quality of cutting comforting, if not slightly obsessive. And from that process, a poem came:

PRACTICE

Pema Norbu Gompo
shares with me a story:
at reaching thirty

thousand prostrations,
glancing into the vanity
to see a trimmed-down waist

w/out love
handles—starting over

from zero, more than
once to better
polish his intent

my own practice:
carving holes in
poetry books w/
exacto blade & straight
edge, intervention as
design concept

a hole too uneven
a hole too big
a hole too ragged
a hole too small

every event a mirror
of mind & heart,
imperfect despite
a template for success,
but isn't there
only this work?

day after day
heaps of words piling
up on my writing desk

▲ *Sightings: Selected Works (2000–2005)*

Book cover by Murillo Design. Hand-cut covers by the author, 1913 Press, 2008.

The cutting reminded me of trimming paper to make handmade books. In the early 2000s, I had enrolled in one of Catherine Papenfoth's papermaking classes and learned to form sheets of paper by breaking down pulp in a blender. It was an easy process that I replicated in my one-bedroom apartment on Beacon Street. The paper lent itself to letter writing and wrapping, but I wanted to do more. In Catherine's bookmaking class, I learned Japanese stitched forms, non-adhesive structures—we sewed decorative papers together with repurposed sketchbook pages. The journals and sketchbooks I made stayed empty—I couldn't bring myself to write in them. They were perfect to me as experiments in form. And while the work of bookmaking and writing happened at the same desk—these practices did not intersect, much like my photography remained independent from my writing.

I was invited to the Provincetown Fine Arts Work Center on a Walker Scholarship. Burned out on creative writing workshops, I signed up for a bookmaking class with Peter Madden. Like Catherine, Peter focused on visual imagery in his book forms, filling them with photographs and prints. But he differed in approaching books as sculptural objects—boxes, triptychs, and cabinets concealed and revealed—to elevate their content. I began to see a connection between text and the physicality of the book. Peter introduced me to many forms—the ox-plow, scrolls, accordion, pop-ups, and folded forms. Studying the shapes of unfolding structures allowed me to visualize an extended poetic line or sequence of texts that could inhabit space with a fullness—I thought of Mei-mei Berssenbrugge's collaborations with Kiki Smith and how her books *Endocrinology* and *Empathy*, even *Four Year Old Girl*, departed radically from the narrow lines of her earliest poems in *The Heat Bird*. Her poems sprawled across page spreads, occupying space in an altogether different way than I had seen poetry do before.

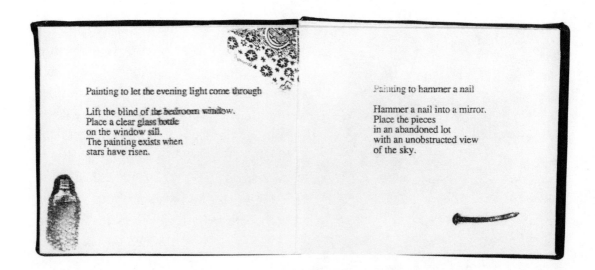

Painting to let the evening light come through

Lift the blind of the bedroom window.
Place a clear glass bottle
on the window sill.
The painting exists when
stars have risen.

Painting to hammer a nail

Hammer a nail into a mirror.
Place the pieces
in an abandoned lot
with an unobstructed view
of the sky.

I laid out my poems "Yes Yoko Ono" and "Poem for [Wolfgang] Laib" into accordion books that summer, incorporating xerox image transfer techniques that I had learned from an alternative photo class. For the "Ono", I selected a dark blue-colored book cloth that evoked Japanese indigo; and for the "Laib", I used paper that conjured the vibrancy of his sculptures constructed from luminous hazelnut pollen. My journals began to look more like sketchbooks, as I mocked up simple structures to bring a different perspective and physicality to a poem—how the poem's final form might not necessarily "lay flat" on the page. In participating in shaping the presentation of my poems through their physical form, I gained a clearer understanding of how I wanted my work to ultimately appear in the world. These early experiences would eventually allow me to imagine a bike trail, a sports field, or an apple orchard as different kinds of literary containers and structures for reading.

I left Peter's workshop with ideas for books that I still dream of making. The ox-plow is a particular form that I continue to return to in my imagination. The shape of the book meanders back and forth in a pattern of cutting and folding that mimics the plowing of a field for planting. Years ago, I thought of harvesting native plants from my father's hometown in rural Taiwan and using those specimens to fabricate sheets of handmade paper. I imagined printing those pages with the stories of my family's histories and making them into an ox-plow book that is still unfolding in my mind.

▲ *Yes Yoko Ono*
Handmade book. Indigo cloth covers on board with accordion structure. Xylene photo transfers. Produced at the Provincetown Fine Arts Work Center, 2003.

▶ **Ox-Plow Book Concept Sketch**
Shin Yu Pai's notebook.

matriarchal line, family curses

women's stories, crones

spirit paper

ancestors + bones

patriarchal line, great grandmother as kung fu master

Qing Ming

burning, ~~spirit paper~~ ignition

setting alight

memorials

grave reorganizing

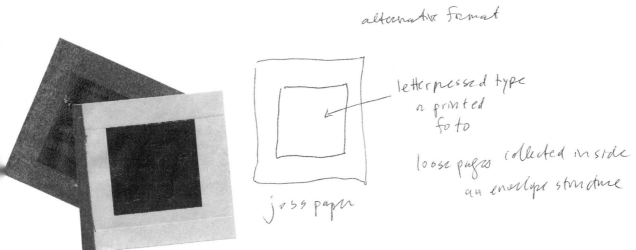

alternative format

letterpressed type a printed foto

loose pages collected inside an envelope structure

joss paper

In graduate school, a classmate approached me about publishing my work. Jerry Tumlinson ran a small DIY press called Third Ear Books. He asked me to pull together a small collection of Chinese poetic translations that I'd been working on with my dad. He'd read the poems in our translation workshop with Anselm Hollo and wanted to circulate them to the larger world. We talked about possible cover designs. Jerry wanted something Asian—a Chinese landscape, a river scene. He knew my mother was a visual artist and suggested that I talk to her about creating something. I had my father translate the assignment for my mother. She made a few sketches drawn in black Sharpie—cartoonish figures in triangular hats scuttling across junk boats. I was baffled by the roughness of her drawings. My mom was a master watercolorist and abstract painter. She confessed later that her art school training in Taipei consisted exclusively of Western and European art. She had no experience in Oriental painting. Her favorite artists were Picasso and Matisse.

Once all the pieces came together, Jerry showed me a single-knot pamphlet stitch. I watched him thread the needle and the drop of blood that emerged from his thumb when he accidentally pricked it. That first blood-smeared copy he held back as "artist proof."

Jerry sewed all 125 copies. And when he was done, we gave most of the books away for free. I remain grateful that he took an early interest in my work, and the object we made together had its own elegance. But I also wondered if the process could have been different. If I could have had more say, if I'd spoken the language of book design. And what a book of my work could be, if I directly shaped the object—if the key actors weren't all white men. If I had taken control of how I wanted the work represented and disrupted the hierarchies of power. Also, I hadn't yet learned to hear the sound of my own voice—which is why I was distracting myself from that work by midwifing a collection of translations in the first place.

I would learn this lesson again in another form—years later, in working with a poetry pub-

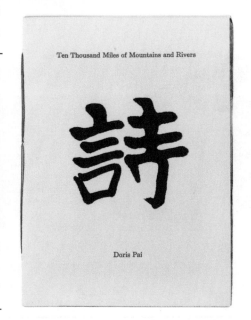

Ten Thousand Miles of Mountains and Rivers

詩

Doris Pai

Ten Thousand Miles of Mountains and Rivers

萬 里 山 河
Translations of Chinese Poetry
by
Doris Pai

Third Ear Books
Boulder, Colorado

Ten Thousand Miles of Mountains and Rivers

▲ Title page. Hand-stitched, washi endpaper. Third Ear Books, Boulder, Colorado, 1998.

◄ Letterpress cover by Brad O'Sullivan of Smokeproof Press. Calligraphy by Keith Kumasen Abbott.

lisher that wanted to move into making more art/text hybrids. The press used my Asian American ethnicity and manuscript in a grant application to the National Endowment for the Arts, which sought to fund new books by "diverse" authors. Except they got it wrong in the application and press release—I wasn't Japanese. My artistic collaborator on the project regretted how his work was visually presented by the publisher's designer, and I did too—the sloppiness of layouts, inconsistencies in backgrounds. The book was ugly, not edgy. And I had no role in the design except to rubber-stamp it and express gratitude. I withdrew the project before the contract was fully executed, but not before being put in my place. The publisher dismissed me as foolish and lectured me on the privilege of having anyone take a vested interest in my work, implying that I was difficult and my work was commercially unviable. The scorn and vitriol over poetry made me feel condemned to never publish again. But I also felt determined to take control over the terms under which I would publish—by partnering with skillful collaborators and being extremely explicit about my vision for a body of

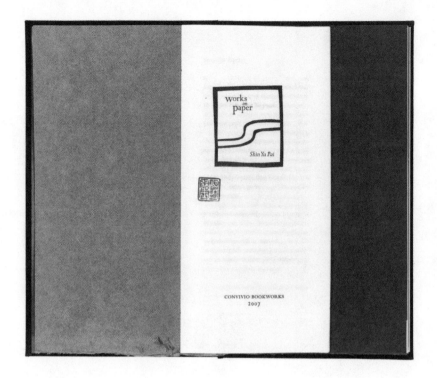

work. I could maintain my commitment to my work by making different choices, namely by closely producing and art-directing the design of my books.

Since those early experiences, I've made different decisions about the kind of relationships I want to have with my publishers and collaborators. I have been fortunate to work with artists and technicians who have included Eliza Wilson-Powers of Press Lorentz, book artists John Cutrone and Seth Thompson of Convivio Bookworks, and Sara Parkel of Filter Press—artists who gave me room to have a voice and vision, to participate in shaping the aesthetic experience of my texts and be a coauthor of that design. Other projects have ranged in their approach, from the undressing of a physical structure to suggest the intimate secrets inherent to a book about Love Hotel poems to a collection of poems about the textures and experience of paper. These physical forms have transformed my work as a poet to create a more complex experience of reading and of a poem. While I may still be searching for a deeper sense of my own voice, I've come to understand that there is also much to be expressed in the embodiment of the idea through the vessel of the book, which itself speaks volumes.

Works on Paper

◄ Handmade Moriki end-paper and title page.

▶ Foldout of "Stars" in *Works on Paper.* Convivio Bookworks, Lake Worth, Florida, 2007.

▼ Sewn on a concertina structure of handmade Fabriano Roma.

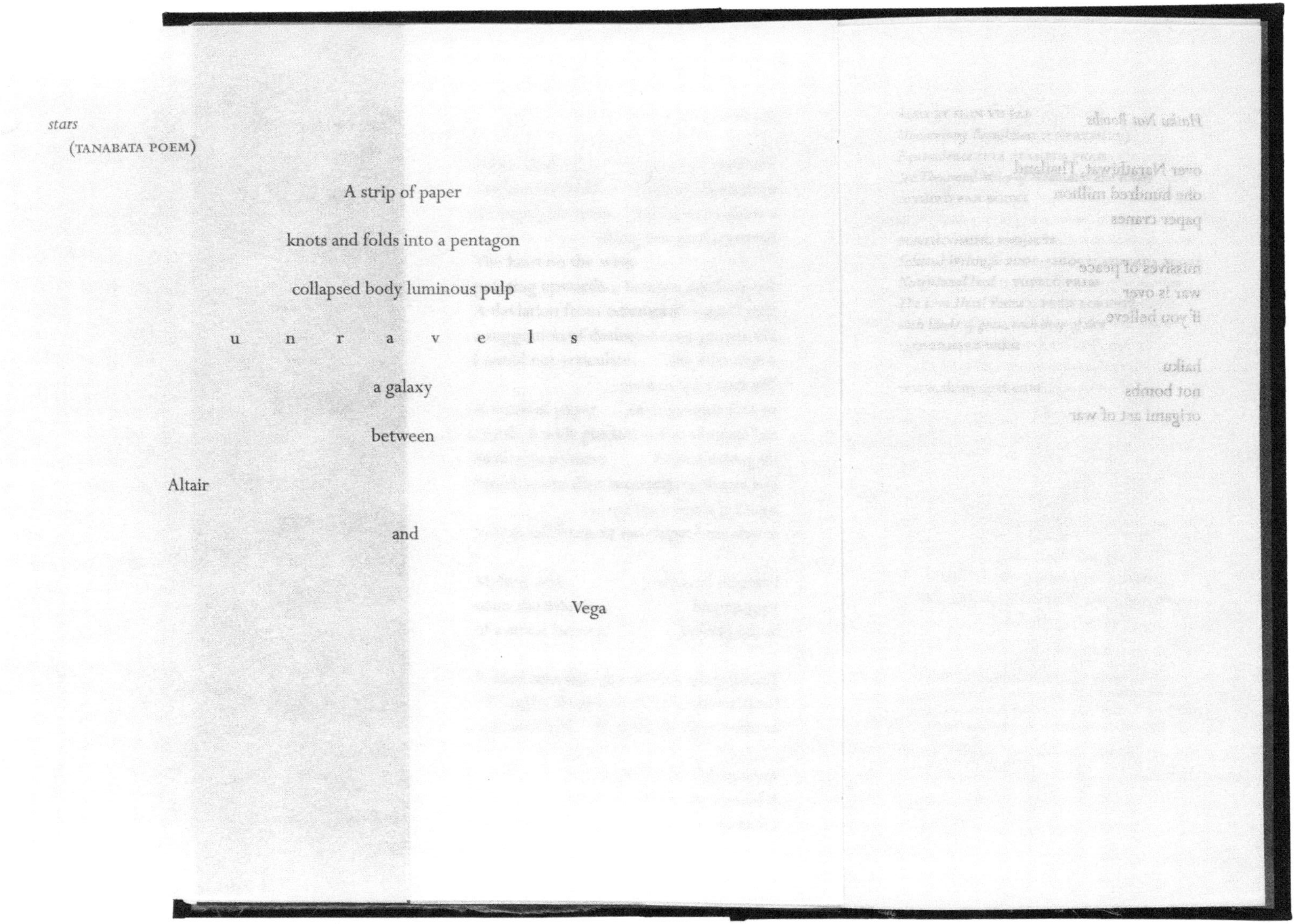

stars
(TANABATA POEM)

A strip of paper

knots and folds into a pentagon

collapsed body luminous pulp

u n r a v e l s

a galaxy

between

and

Altair

Vega

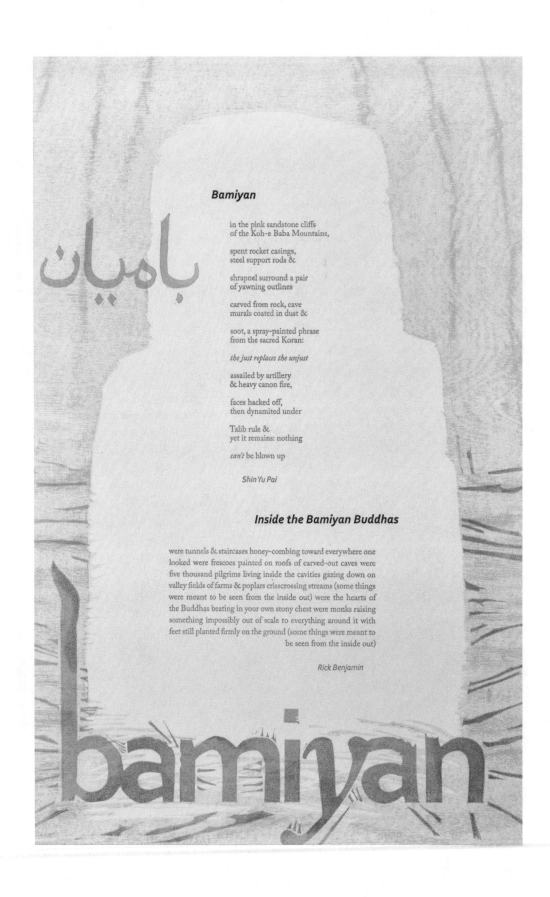

Bamiyan

in the pink sandstone cliffs
of the Koh-e Baba Mountains,

spent rocket casings,
steel support rods &

shrapnel surround a pair
of yawning outlines

carved from rock, cave
murals coated in dust &

soot, a spray-painted phrase
from the sacred Koran:

the just replaces the unjust

assailed by artillery
& heavy canon fire,

faces hacked off,
then dynamited under

Talib rule &
yet it remains: nothing

can't be blown up

Shin Yu Pai

Inside the Bamiyan Buddhas

were tunnels & staircases honey-combing toward everywhere one
looked were frescoes painted on roofs of carved-out caves were
five thousand pilgrims living inside the cavities gazing down on
valley fields of farms & poplars crisscrossing streams (some things
were meant to be seen from the inside out) were the hearts of
the Buddhas beating in your own stony chest were monks raising
something impossibly out of scale to everything around it with
feet still planted firmly on the ground (some things were meant to
be seen from the inside out)

Rick Benjamin

70

◂ **"Bamiyan" broadside with Rick Benjamin**

Designed and printed by Filter Press, Gordo, Alabama, 2009.

▸ *Hybrid Land*

Collagraph pressure printing, woodcuts, photopolymer, wood type. Bamboo covers with silk-screen title. Ethiopian-style link-stitch binding. Printed by Sara Parkel at Filter Press, Gordo, Alabama, 2011.

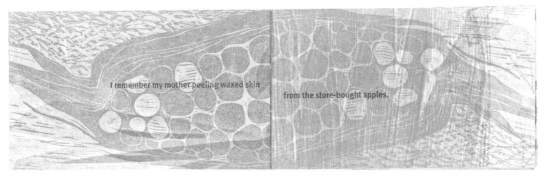

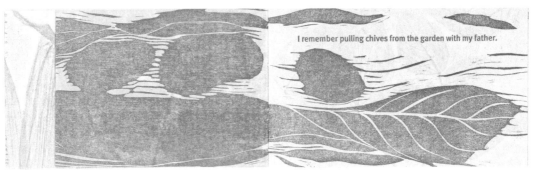

HYBRID LAND

recall Country Crock

recall Ocean Mist

recall Frontera

recall Nestlé

recall SanLu

recall Campbell

recall Kellogg

recall Kroger

I remember by mother peeling waxed skins from store-bought fruit.

I remember apples we grew—their skins, dull, form misshapen.

I remember holes pecked by bird beaks scarring unripe peaches.

I remember the sweet stink of guavas rotting on the earth.

I remember pulling chives from the garden with my father.

I remember homegrown loofah gourds drying in sun.

I remember the family dog shaded by grape arbor.

I remember a baby slug leeched onto bright red strawberry.

recall beefsteak

recall capsicum

recall alfalfa

recall savoy

recall groundnut

recall pistachio

recall white bread

recall chicken egg

THE LOVE HOTEL POEMS

Shin Yu Pai

The Love Hotel Poems

▲ Title page, hand-sewn with found advertisements. Everywhere Godfrey Series for Press Lorentz, Chicago, 2006.

▸ Interior cover detail.

CONSOLE

				channel	lolicon		
hello	kitty						space
	holiday				rated	gen	X
	times			five	★★★★★		familiar
		love	hotel		away	from	home

DIRTY

in the aftermath of love-

making the bed, stripping
sweat-soaked sheets

the unmentionable

details of a family-
owned operation,

an obasan sanitizes
the spanking horse

while a grandmother
tidies rooms, rows

of empty spines

behind the scenes
a pair of liver-spotted

hands taking a key

MOTHERING TIME

In the gesture of my son's hand curling to imitate
the tightly furled fern, the poetry that reaches
beyond language.

GIVING BIRTH

Becoming a mother entered my heart for the first time at a funeral parlor in Montreal. The Alfred Dallaire Memoria is a minimalist space with soaring ceilings that evokes a gallery more than a mortuary:

> It is not easy to hold back
> what's known once a thing
> has risen into the world
> it can weigh each day a little longer

The poet Peter Eihei Levitt, an ordained Zen priest, told of becoming a father for the second time in his fifties. Already the parent to a grown, adult daughter, Peter hadn't planned on raising more children. But he met a younger woman whom he fell in love with and married. She wanted a child; he didn't. Eventually, the Zen poet awakened to the depth of his wife's longing. He gazed into his heart and asked himself, "Who am I to deny her this experience?"

In his poem, the face of a childhood friend pressed against a window transmutes into the poet's wife dreaming the face of their unborn son. By the time Peter finished reading, I couldn't stop weeping.

I'd been with my partner for ten years. I'd never wanted to have a child, but fatherhood was something that he strongly desired. The idea that we could have a family together suddenly took hold.

My career as an arts administrator delayed the opportunity to more seriously consider having children. But this also gave me the time to come to an emotionally neutral place about becoming

a mother. On a planned detox, after leaving a particularly fly-by-night pseudoacademic job, I consulted with an Ayurvedic vaidya about verified fertility issues only to be told by her I was "too old" and that I "better hurry up." Her commentary was not much better than my Western doctor, who let me know the "problem" was not in fact my biology, but my husband's motility. I ditched all medical advice in favor of the vision that came to me following a netra basti treatment, a therapy that opens and ignites the crown chakra and stimulates the third eye. I had hopes of deeper insight, while literally nourishing the eyes, of also awakening the intuition within. The treatment involves having a volcano of dough constructed around one eye at a time, which is then filled with oil. The eye opens inside the lake of ghee and is exercised by a series of subtle movements.

As I lay with eyes closed on the treatment table after having both eyes cleansed, my mother drifted up out of my consciousness, radiant and full of love. A love that I had never seen. Two things were true: When I was born, she looked upon me with absolute love; and that this love that appeared to me was not simply my mother's love, but the source of all maternal love.

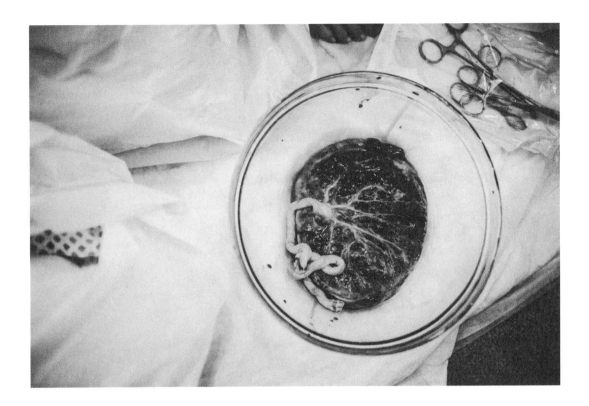

Months later, I conceived a child whom I lost.

Instead of grief, I had duty. I had agreed to travel with my father back to Taiwan to sites that haunted him, the places of his military services, his hometown. I bore witness to his story, to understand the legacy of who we are, even as I did not give myself the solitude needed to process my own grief. To dwell in this darkness was to gather up and hold the memories of my father's younger self. To accept the duties of firstborn son, as my father's traveling companion, but to also take on a role that I hadn't expected—mother to the wounded parts that he had turned away from. I returned from the trip depleted and saddened by the trauma of my father's history and my own experience of denying myself the solitude needed to process my loss.

My neutrality grew into sadness.

It was a surprise to conceive again quickly and an experience that I could not fully trust. Some women love pregnancy—but for me carrying a child was a profound experience of being alone, not unlike being a writer. My difficulty with trusting the process, the anxiety and fear of failure, were mine to bear alone. Yet my

pregnancy developed predictably, and, ten days before my due date, I went into labor after reading poems for my neighborhood library. My son entered the world at 7:26 a.m. on September 13, 2013, in a midwife-assisted unmedicated home birth. He was born with the caul, a remnant of the amniotic sac, that clung to his head and concealed his face from first view. I literally did not leave my house for weeks—my son, Tomo, became the center of my life.

After giving birth, I started paying attention to time. I tracked the intervals between feedings, bowel movements, and naps. I turned my attention to developmental stages, the coming in of teeth—watching for the proper time to introduce food. I tracked my son's language development, which would be two years delayed. I did not have time to think about making art or writing. I gave up reading novels and poetry for books on childhood development. Motherhood was not intuitive.

Then something shifted. We'd begun taking long walks in Carkeek Park, and discovered an heirloom fruit orchard on the land. We picked the fruit, and I noticed how my son clasped and played with the apples. I'd been planning on doing a project in the orchard, but completely reimagined my approach based on wanting to make a work for my son that he might understand and appreciate. Though I tended to eschew form, I chose to write an abecedarian to give my ideas structure. I'd stepped away from creative thought for so long that form finally made intuitive sense. The poems were short and grounded in the site-specific details of the land, which helped me to reenter imaginative space after having been so distant from that place.

In expanding the audience of my work to my young son, how I thought about my work changed. I grew less interested in writing for the page and more interested in taking risks that could make my work available to people outside of the typical audience of poetry. I wanted to see the poetry that is everywhere around us through my son's eyes and to activate that space. My work wasn't durational in the past, but I now pay attention deeply to time—the hours of sunlight in a day necessary to make a chlorophyll print; the duration of days to imprint a ripening apple; the length of almost twenty years to finish a series about an art gallery—themes repeating themselves, looping like an animation.

I fully expected motherhood to be obliterating. The end of myself as I knew me. What I didn't anticipate was the expansion that my spirit would undergo to integrate all of the parts of my previous identities to make me a better human and mother.

When I observe my son, I feel a kind of primal life force and intuitive creativity at play, a burning curiosity about his relationship to the people and things in his world. How he rhymes the word "placenta" with "Santa," taking measured pleasure in language—the apple never falling far from the tree.

DIVIDING
THE MILK

Sunday morning before
my son stirs, I divide
the milk for banking

bag seven ounces
for the icebox put
aside a shot glass full

for an offering

～

in one temple's ritual
reenactment milk

is flushed down a drain
water returning to water—

hundreds of schoolkids
drowned when the ferry

went down, a white line
of lanterns coiling

down a river
single wave forms

returning to sea

～

inside the ceramic
bowl a jizo sits

awaiting activation,
guardian of lost

children—picture
a puja, a milk bath

a cleansing

~

ceremony centering
on feeding the spirit

a paper stand-in
for the unborn

baby—without a body,
what kinship looks

like when there is
no way to nurse

the human form reduced
to diamonds and triangles

cells dividing

~

black marker outlining
lifelike features

the lips of a hand-drawn
face, grow translucent

when touched by dampness
feeding the baby a metaphor

I fold an ordinary leaf
baptized in a bottle of milk,

cup the edge to a corner
of the figure's mouth

thinking of how my body
has sustained the life

of my infant son each
day since his birth

I feed the doll three times,
when Kort touches its face,

the dummy slumps forward

~

the effigy is burned
before its ashes

are scooped up, entombed
inside the buddha

some parents
undertake action to

lay the spirit of the unborn
babe to rest—to stop

the spirit from disturbing
the sleep of a younger

sibling, Tomo our second
child, when we leave

the building he can't stop
wailing, sleeps deep

that night as the dead

~

when he turns to face us,
the priest showers handfuls

of paper flowers, raining
down above the heads

of my boy, my husband,
& me, sakura petal, moth

wings, an explosion
of blossoms marking

the moment of release

~

the cleric's robes conceal
the cremation from view,

flint striking steel
paper ignites into flame

the burning body banished
from sight, a plastic spoon

scoops out remains

in pregnancy, a healer once
warned avoiding violence,

coming into contact with a corpse
l stop watching the evening

news: turn away from
police tape & bloodied

rolls of gauze staining
the concrete at Third & Pine

~

my body bled
for twenty-eight days,
this slow letting go

the Swedish midwife
described the expulsion
of tissue as a medical

event, a process
no worse than a "heavy
period," the blighted ovum

versus a life cut short
babes, aborted fetuses,
sucked out in the same

breath put next to
the choice to take an untested
drug intended to treat ulcers

to rupture the uterus

~

I dress the jizo
in a red cape &

felt hat, tuck
handwritten messages

from his father & me
into the inside of its coat

a week earlier
I am flippant when

I tell him to write
a letter to our "dead baby";

at the last minute
I question both

his salutation & sign off

anxious he'll find
the task uninspired

before the mizuko kuyo
I spy his note inside

the jizo's box, beside
a toy top, a box of rice

candy saved from our wedding
nine years ago, sweet

comfort to offer a child
unfolding yellow paper

to read in my partner's
precise hand, "Dear Baby,

I am sorry I was not
more welcoming—may you
find the love you need"

your father
your mother

HEIRLOOM

We encounter the same objects, day after day,
walk the same paths, eat the same food, form
relationships to what is familiar. What happens
when we look deeper to ask how our surround-
ings came into being? How might that alter our
relationship to time?

THE POETRY AROUND US

In the late 1990s, I spent long hours in the photo lab at the School of the Art Institute of Chicago pulling prints from chemical baths and learning to see pure blacks and details in the greys. The emergence of the image beneath the red safelights had its magic, but I hated working in the dark. The environment of the lab exacerbated my poor eyesight, and I worried about the toxic load of working around chemicals. My pregnant classmate started wearing a full-face respirator. A professor, who'd spent decades in the darkroom, shared her terminal diagnosis with colleagues. These factors colored my attitude towards darkroom work, and, eventually, I would give up printing. I longed for a process that would allow me to see the image directly revealed in light, without any need for safelights.

In 2012, on a hike to the beach near our Seattle home, I came across an open meadow planted with apple, pear, and nut trees. Piper's Orchard, as it's known, was established by early European settlers, and the land around it is now a city park. The few signs posted by the parks department showed a rough map of tree species and alluded with skeletal detail to the history of the land and to Andrew and Minna Piper—the homesteaders who created the orchard. I was intrigued by the mysterious grove—how it got there, who maintained it, and its heirloom strains of fruit.

A few weeks after my encounter with this orchard, an article came out in the *New York Times* about an apple engineered in such a way that, when cut into, the flesh would not go brown from exposure to oxygen. Years earlier, I'd written a series of poems exploring food and agricultural themes in a project called *Nutritional Feed*. So these types of stories tend to capture my interest.

Over the years, a group of curators and artists have organized ongoing site-specific art installations in Carkeek Park. As I walked through Piper's Orchard, I recalled an orchard in Japan that tattooed its apples with kanji, up-selling them as artisanal products. It seemed to me that the apples, and the orchard then in its entirety, could function as a giant light-sensitive surface. Why not print a poem on an apple? Or parts of it? The exploration of genetically modified food seemed like a natural extension of that previous work. The piece could be made more poignant by printing sections of the poem on the ripening apples of the trees. I consulted a tree steward to ask if he thought sun prints could work and embarked on a pilot to test the idea.

I made a series of prints over the summer of 2014. As different apple varieties rolled into ripeness—Wealthy, Astrachan, and Dutch Mignonne—I applied decals on selected species and let the letters burn in over the course of seven to ten days. There was a lot of trial and error to find the right printing substrate, and it was necessary to cultivate deep patience in order to wait the weeks needed to see what worked and what failed, an experience with making art that I had not had before.

My son, Tomo, frequently came with me to the orchard during my field visits and printing tests. I watched my young child toddle through the meadow, picking and eating apples from the trees with the help of my husband. Tomo was learning to walk and just beginning to explore talking. I thought about how language could be made more visible and delightful to a child encountering words for the first time. And as I reflected on my child's experiences, I realized everything I wanted to say in my poem could take the form of a field guide for visitors—for families—a text that could teach my son everything that I wanted him to know about Piper's Orchard: the fruit trees, the land, and the people who'd cared for it. Minna Piper, the mother of eleven children, had been credited historically with grafting the varietals. And it's her name, and not her husband's, that appears in my poem.

Heirloom evolved into the shape of a twenty-six section abecedarian, or alphabet poem, with each section taking a separate letter of the alphabet as its starting point. In 2015, I reentered the orchard with words from my completed poem that I had laser cut as custom decals. I removed the white bags and nylon socks protecting the fruit from the apple maggots and burnished the letters into place with a bone folder. In each tree, I stenciled a specific grouping of words and repeated this process over several weekends with various trees.

Strangers picked and devoured the stickered apples, leaving behind the evidence of unripe, gnawed apple cores. Summer storms took down the fruit. I found artfully arranged, stenciled fruit in piles around tree trunks. Where the apples did stay on the branch, I'd return to peel away the decals to reveal the pale green words written in the trees. When further exposed to the sun, these areas reddened and reverted to their natural tendencies. Because I always knew that the installation would be overtaken by nature and endure for only a short period, I asked my friend Tom Stiles, who is an audio engineer at Jack Straw Cultural Center, to capture audio field recordings in the orchard throughout the different seasons. He recorded birdsong, the sound of wind moving through the meadow, tree stewards mulching the orchard, and apple fall.

A volunteer tree steward collected fallen apples to press cider and sent me a cell phone photo of an apple emblazoned with the word BOUNTY, before he juiced the fruit. I began to give up control of my collaboration with nature to nature. The elements erased whatever language I tried to record and recompose, and by the end of apple season, I'd come to terms with the idea that I could not control anything about the poem. I had shaped the text on the page, but fidelity to the place that inspired it meant letting the piece live differently in the real world. My words belonged to me, but once they entered the public space, I no longer owned them.

In the course of my research about Piper's Orchard, I learned that apple orchards are often wassailed, or sung to, by the people that maintain the land in order to ensure a good harvest. I think of *Heirloom* as a ballad that sings the stories of Piper's—snapshots combining with sounds collected from the land to capture the textures and colors of a place, long after the apples have gone to seed.

ANTIQUE   freckled, scabbed &
             spotted Astrachans
             ushered from Russia
             heritage strains older
             than the Arctic©

BOUNTY   gleaned & given
             thousands of pounds
             of unsellable fruit
             circulate to city
             food banks

CANOPY   arbors full of stars
             five-pointed calyxes
             scoring undersides
             of apples

(RED) DELICIOUS   "Stark's Hawkeye"
             stocking grocers thick-
             skinned, overgrown
             bred for its hue, "retains
             its cheerful good looks
             long after its flavor has departed"
             —mealy mouthfeel of
             an American classic

EYE   apple
                 of my

FOUND   beneath ivy & thorn,
              arching cane & suckering
              root, ruin—the forest orchard
              "gone to seed"

GRAFTAGE   tree cuttings
              implanted into host
              stumps sealed w/ wax
              to propagate a vanishing line

HEIRLOOM   belonging passed
              between generations
              a historic homestead
              a grove of fruit-bearing trees
              totems of memory—an apple,
              all the way from Denmark

INDEX

JEFFERSON'S   favorite: the orange
Pippin sweeter with age
vulnerable to cankers &
fire blights, subtle
russeting

KEEPSAKE   apples prized
for their profile &
flavor, revival of
heritage fruit, genome
splicing, giving flower
to centuries-old
species

LORE   heirs of the wild
apples of Tian Shan,
celestial peaks, producers
of the Almaty,
"Alma-Ata"—almighty
Kazakh Father
of Apples carried
along the Silk Road
in the bellies of beasts

MINNA   Wilhemina Piper
         (Pfeifer), master
         gardener, mother
         to eleven, planted
         seedlings at "The Ranch"
         handpicked apples
         folded into strudel at
         her husband's konditorei
         the sweetshop burned
         to the ground, twenty-five
         city blocks lost
         to the Great Fire

NONESUCH   names like "woolfibbers"

Ozark Gold

Golden Gem

Pound Sweet

Sheepnose

Chenango Strawberry

Piñata

Api Etoile

Pixie Crunch

Winter Banana

Hidden Rose

Spokane Beauty

Maiden's Blush

American Mother

Moneycrisp

ORIGIN   story: family outings

to Apple Country, Oak Glen

nestled in the foothills of

The San Bernardino Mountains—

at the top of the scenic loop,

I tasted flavors out of hand

Ben Davis, Gravenstein,

Pink Pearl though my father

always took home the sack

of coke-shaped hawkeyes

candy red & sweet

still big in Asia

PARENTS   chance seedlings

"the apple doesn't fall

far from the tree"

QR

SCION   wood entwined w/
rootstock sprouts new
offshoots form vascular
connections, limbs
lifting up living
tissue, cambium green

TOAST   work parties in the woods
stewards impale browned
bread to branches, singers
serenading the orchard
"toast" to its health

URBAN(E)   artisan sparkling
ciders & wines
fermented from
heirloom crop
public food
forest for
the foraging
a bouquet of apples

VOLUNTEER   rogue seed scattered
by bird droppings, vintage stripe
springing forth

WASSAIL

Blow, blow bear well
spring well in April.
Every sprig, and every spray
bear a bushel of apples
against next New Year's Day!

Health to thee
good apple tree
well to bear
pockets full, hats full
bushel bags full
pecks full, hats full
caps full bushel
bushel sacks full
and my pockets too.
Huzzah!

Stand fast root
bear well top
pray God send us
a good howling crop
every twig, apples big
every bough, apples enow.

Hats full, caps full
full quarter sacks full
holla, boys, holla!

EXOCARP   fleshy fruit
hypanthium
floral cup
corolla forming
edible outer layer

YIELD   two types of windfall:
zephyr & plenty
giving under gentle
pressure, tender
to the touch

SPITZ   Doppelgänger of the Westfield
seek-no-further—yellow mottled
dots against an orange-red
backdrop, one of four kinds
raised at Monticello
predating the American Revolution

SAME CLOTH

Reclaiming the materiality of the textile was a means of subverting the static quality of the printed page to evoke the language of lived trauma and to make that pain tactile and visible.

THE ROLE OF POETRY

Scanning the daily headlines, I encounter a story about an incident on Seattle's east side. A black business owner who runs a consignment shop discovers a Klan robe. A woman named Leona Coakley-Spring finds a Ku Klux Klan robe left at her store in Redmond. In the suburbs of Seattle, someone leaves a racist robe for someone else to find.

Is it a hate crime?

She opens a bag left by a brown-haired white man in his twenties, and there it is. An investigation ensues. She decides to close her shop. *There is no justice.*

Is it a hate crime?

When the investigation ends, the police return the evidence. She sets the robe afire. This is the news I consume.

How should a city react? What is my responsibility as a poet and as the poet laureate of that city to raise my voice? I was navigating new terrain—my creativity had previously always been mine to own, but the sensitivities of working with a municipal government affected my ability to be completely effective in my role. I thought deeply about how one can publicly address wounds in the community born of injustice and intergenerational trauma.

The Confederate flag went up on my neighbors' balcony two days after my husband and I moved into our apartment in San Marcos, Texas. The timing seemed conspicuous, but I convinced myself that

I was overthinking our college-aged neighbors' choice of decor. The flag occupied a place on the spectrum of covert racism, but distant from the more frightening white hoods and burning crosses. We had to live next door to it for a year—so why make a fuss?

Is it more than a microaggression?

A friend comes to visit and shoves a shaky hand through thick rows of braids and under her breath asks, "How do you feel about living next to that…?"

The flag is a code. The South is full of them, sometimes not as obvious.

An acquaintance may smile and say, "Bless your heart," but mean, "Sweet Lord, you idiot." Which is how the manager of the apartment complex responded when I finally worked up the nerve to complain. "Bless your heart"—she reasoned it was like pride in a sports team, pride in your heritage. If we were to ban the Confederate flag, then wouldn't we have to take down the flags of soccer fans expressing their enthusiasm for the Chinese or Brazilian teams?

The next day, the neighbor added three new items to his outdoor decoration—a ceramic "welcome" sign, a doormat proclaiming friendship, and a pair of bright blue Chinese paper lanterns that swung above the battle flag. A crisp, new Confederate bandana hung from the rearview mirror of his pickup.

Is it more than aggression?

We break our lease eight months later. An opportunity to leave Texas arose, and we jumped at it. By the time I walked across the parking lot to give notice, I was once again emotional about the racist flag I'd had to walk by every day and the way the apartment manager casually brushed off my concern; it's just like a sports team.

The people I loved felt unsafe visiting.
People I loved felt unsafe. I felt unsafe.
It was not neutral.

It was harm.

My heart felt lighter the minute we left San Marcos to find our new home—but that first weekend away ended with a menacing message in my work inbox.

Subject: Our flag
From: unknown sender <confederateflag2010@yahoo.com>

I clicked on the message:

No matter how many white guys you fuck, you will never be white. If you say anything again about our flag, we will take you down. Watch out!

How had they gotten my work email? We'd only ever exchanged first names. Was I being cyberstalked? Did they follow me to work?

The officer took my statement, wrote down a case number on a blue card, and told me I'd hear back in a week. When several weeks passed, I called the number on the card. Investigators had traced the email to a computer in a science building at UCLA. From there, of course, the trail went cold.

On a late Thursday afternoon, Detective Duwayne Poorboy knocked on my door. He questioned the neighbors and decided they were "good old country boys," much like himself—incapable of orchestrating a complicated plan involving the Internet. Towering above me at six feet tall in his uniform, Detective Poorboy asserted, "In these parts, the Confederate flag just doesn't mean what it means to y'all up north."

The "boys" blushed when confronted with the sexist language of the message that had been sent to me. Poorboy empathized with the young men, who were terrified they could lose their housing or get kicked out of school—it could ruin their lives. The roommates had stopped trusting each other, unsure of who was telling the truth. And, in reality, the culprits could have been one of the neighbors' girlfriends, or our downstairs neighbor, a sorority girl, who my husband regularly confronted over her drinking and loud parties.

Is it a hate crime?

There was no neutrality in Detective Poorboy, who was fully focused on relieving the discomfort and suffering of my white neighbors. The flag was moved several feet back from the balcony to cover the window of the neighbors' apartment. Whenever one of the neighbors saw me in the parking lot, he'd gun his engine loudly and tear by, as if to run me down.

Is it a hate crime?

I wrote the poem "Same Cloth" in reaction to what happened to Leona Coakley-Spring. Though the symbols were different, I understood that the intimidation had lasting repercussions. When I lived in Texas, I didn't have the power or safety to respond.

I wrote the poem within the week of reading the story, as an act of solidarity. That was in 2016. The City held me back from circulating it until 2017. I discussed with parks department staff sharing it as part of Black History Month or other possible opportunities, but the fact that the investigation was ongoing and that the poem included details of the crime made the piece off-limits. In the meantime, I reimagined what the piece could become. I wanted a physical object that could reclaim the cloth and invoke a visceral experience. A concrete remembrance that could invite a deeper reflection on the impact of doing others harm.

Leona burned the robe before I had thought to ask to use it for my public art project on hatred. My peers in the community thought working in canvas to replicate the robe might open new wounds rather than heal. That a different, lighter medium might widen a different space of possibility. This dialogue with the community guided my selection of silk organza—a delicate fabric with a soft transparency—and blood red thread to symbolize human connection. The light through the fabric made the red stitching all that more intense.

While writing "Same Cloth" didn't minimize the trauma in my early life, it felt like a transgressive act. A way to revisit a wound that I needed to move beyond in order to take up space anew.

And rectify being made invisible so many years ago.

▶ **Same Cloth**

Embroidered broadside. Cotton thread on silk organza. Commissioned by the City of Redmond, Washington. 2017.

same cloth

a poem for Leona Coakley-Spring

the white robe, a length of rope
a pointed hat: hate symbols
evidence of a message much
louder than "go back to where
you came from,"

there are people here who will hurt you
a veiled threat that burns
bright as any wooden cross
planted in the earth as if
to stake a claim, what if we
were to sow seeds of
solidarity for a stranger
public victims of a hate crime
the "black business owner"
who believed the best about
another human — instead
of recognizing the glory suit
for its cut out eye holes
saw a choir robe
to sing the holy gospel
to know this neighbour
by her name, to recover
some deeper meaning of "clan"

WITHOUT
WORDS

ON INEFFABILITY

How does the story of a place or a person slip into the historical record? Poring over a century's worth of images at a local archive, I thought about this question. As I sifted through records and artifacts collected by the Redmond Historical Society, I read the stories of Skid Row in the portraits of mill workers—traced the disappearance of the city's woodlands as they were harvested. I looked into the faces of pale ancestors, searching for people who might look like me, thinking about the diversity of immigrants who occupy the land today and make it their home.

Memory resides in the land. My attention turned towards the environment, in my attempt to better understand a quality of place, beyond cultural history. I harvested leaves from local plants. With these samples in hand, I took the images that I culled from the historical archive and used them to make a series of chlorophyll prints. Attending over the printing process beneath the summer sun, I watched these images develop over hours and days—the slow writing of the image burned in by light.

I made images of the city's logging industry, its agricultural past, and civic celebrations on hosta, ginkgo, and blackberry leaves. As the sun bleached out the chlorophyll from each surface, the individual variations of the leaves imbued each historical image with a living, breathing quality.

The printed image continues to degrade—evolving, dynamic. They invoke a poetic gesture between a seen history and the land, while invoking what perhaps is forgotten or invisible. I allow them to decompose as a reminder that nothing is fixed, all is impermanent. Even as a historic image is brought to life again, it recedes.

ANIMATING THE TEXT

I'm interested in the idea of being "in time" with a poem as it emerges and comes alive. Being in this liminal space before an audience becomes less about performance and more about connection, to one's self and within the context of a larger public or humanity.

COMING ALIVE

When we bring poetry into the space of civic gatherings, we ask so much of it. We expect it to bring people together, to unite us through lyric experience. The crowd in front of me wanted Christmas carols and holiday lights, not to listen to poetry. And though the public played a hand in sourcing the ideas and lines that made up my poem—I felt a profound sense of disconnection.

Since making *Heirloom*, I've been more interested in the interplay of environment and text. I surrender my attachment to the control afforded by the written page to bring poems into a world they can inhabit, while being shaped by chance. Some of my recent projects ask how poems can be presented without me delivering their reading—I explore what it feels like to take my physicality offstage. To remove myself as go-between or vehicle of connection in order to encourage direct experience.

I'd had a long history of creating visual and shaped poems in projects like "Unnecessary Roughness" and "Nutritional Feed"— poems that guided a reader's eye across the page using forms drawn from recognizable visual cues like play diagrams and nutritional labels. Animation expanded this visual approach by introducing movement to illuminate the text. While I set out to create a poetic experience that an audience might not expect, by bringing a new dimension to previously static work, I found new challenges and unexpected opportunities.

My project, *heyday*, draws its inspiration from urban forestry in cities built out of clear-cuts—the story of the Northwest. I knew from the start that I wanted to project this poem as large as possible and made a plan to do so on the back of Redmond's City Hall during

cedar felled fir

1.

to create
the city's
earliest trade;

2.

timber

timber

3.

with logs rolled, skidded
down roads to arrive

4.

at a new understory,

what a
sampling of
sylvae

5.

one thousand acres to be brought
into active trust — the city of tree
stewards recover a watershed,

6.

cultivate urban vegetation,
extend the forest canopy

7.

to change the temperature

8.

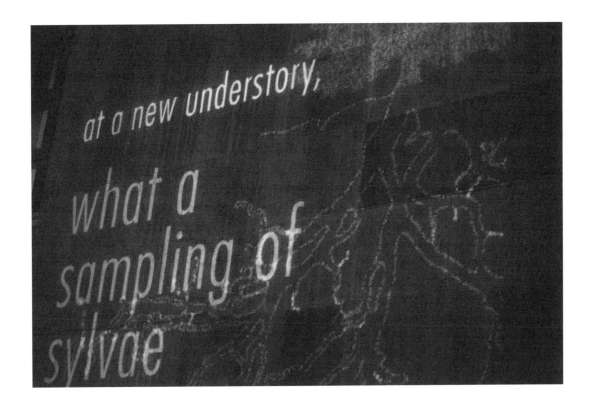

heyday

▲ Projection with Michael Barakat. Commissioned by the City of Redmond, Washington, 2017.

◄ Stills from *heyday* animation.

a winter festival. But to do this, I also needed to find someone who could help bring my vision to reality.

Michael Barakat is a graphic designer and animator in Seattle, who is also a musician and maker of bespoke shoes. I knew that I could bring Michael visual examples of the strategies I wanted to pursue and open up a conversation. We looked at visual poems by Guillaume Apollinaire and Ian Hamilton Finlay. I'd seen an animated text piece drawn from the language from a historical lynching poster by Seattle artist Paul Rucker, which pointed me towards an approach that could privilege the text and simultaneously re-appropriate it as image.

I wanted to create a text-based animation with minimal additional visual imagery to focus explicitly on the experience of reading. Drawing from the strategies in the concrete poem examples I'd shared with him, Michael mocked up a simple storyboard where the words of my poems took the shape of fallen logs, root networks, and visual references to trees.

As I watched the winter sky darken, the projected image slowly grew more intricate. Illuminated words danced across the three-story building. It was nothing less than magical to see my poem about the history of the land echo off of a concrete wall so far removed from the natural past.

Around this period, I wrapped up my professional tenure with Amplifier, an activist nonprofit design firm. It made headlines in early 2017 for its "We the People" campaign, which hacked the presidential inauguration by purchasing full-page ad space in the *New York Times* and the *Washington Post* to circulate activist art used by marchers in the much larger Women's March the following day. Amplifier's approach focuses on creative distribution and space hacking: taking over empty walls and public space with unsanctioned protest art, while sourcing its best ideas and images from the community.

Puget Sound Driftwood Circle took what I learned from *heyday* and the design processes used at Amplifier and turned my attention towards a new collaboration with a community. Once again, I knew I wanted to work with a building-scaled project, but this time, I'd arrange lines given to me by others.

The piece is a collaborative response to Richard Long's sculpture of the same name, which was on display at the Henry Art Gallery, as part of the exhibition *The Time. The Place*. Long's works naturally invite deeper reflection—he often assembles local and found materials, like driftwood or stone, into minimalist sculptural works. I was teaching a poetry workshop on ekphrastic writing in the galleries and asked each student to write two lines contemplating the driftwood in Long's piece. Where did it come from? How did it get there?

I created two versions of the poem—a narrative text with line breaks; and a second version that combined the verses into a visual poem which mimicked the shape and form of actual driftwood arranged into a floor piece. I asked my *heyday* collaborator, Michael,

Puget Sound Driftwood Circle

▲ Richard Long, *Puget Sound Driftwood Circle*, 1996, driftwood, 116 in. (294.6 cm) length of longest piece of driftwood; 276 in. (701 cm) or 300 in. (762 cm) variable diameter, Henry Art Gallery, University of Washington, Seattle.
▶ *Puget Sound Driftwood Circle* collaboration with Michael Barakat and workshop participants.

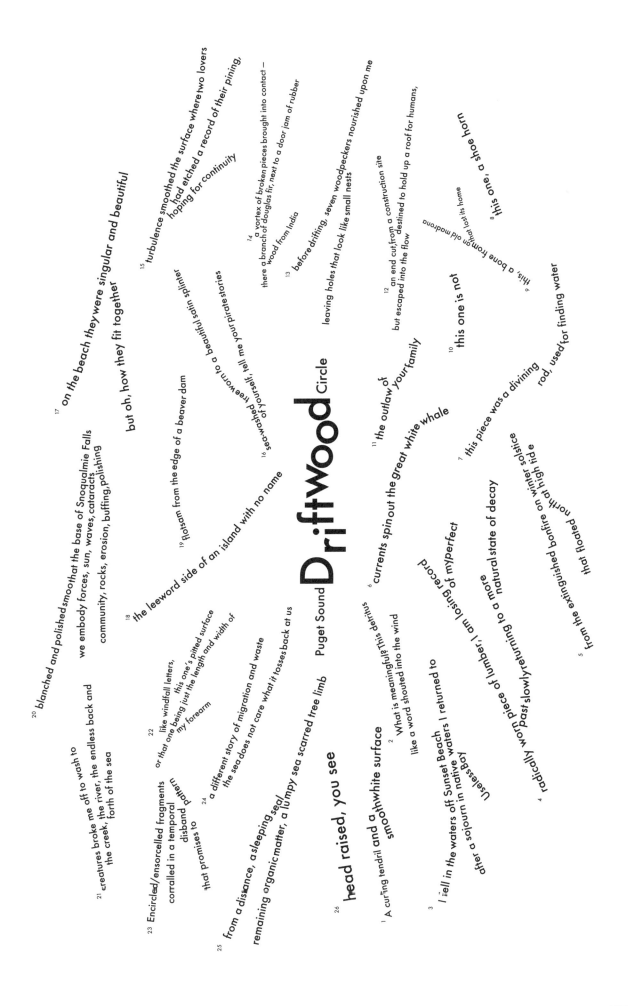

Driftwood Circle

Puget Sound

1 A curling tendril and a smooth white surface

2 What is meaningful? This detritus / like a word shouted into the wind

3 I fell in the waters off Sunset Beach I returned to / after a sojourn in native waters Bay / Useless Bay

4 radically worn piece of lumber, I am losing to a more / natural state of decay

5 from the extinguished bonfire on winter solstice / north, that floated past slowly returning to / that floated north at high tide

6 currents spin out the great white whale

7 this piece was a divining

8 this one, a shoe horn

9 this, a bone from an old madrona that lost its home

10 this one is not

11 the outlaw of your family

12 an end cut from a construction site / but escaped into the flow / destined to hold up a roof for humans,

13 before drifting, seven woodpeckers nourished upon me / leaving holes that look like small nests

14 a vortex of broken pieces brought into contact — / there a branch of douglas fir, next to a door jam of rubber / wood from India

15 turbulence smoothed the surface where two lovers / had etched a record of their pining, / hoping for continuity

16 sea-washed tree worn to / of yourself, tell me your pirate stories / a beautiful satin splinter

17 on the beach they were singular and beautiful

18 the leeword side of an island with no name

19 flotsam from the edge of a beaver dam

20 blanched and polished smooth that the base of Snoqualmie Falls

21 creatures broke me off to wash to / we embody forces, sun, waves, cataracts / the creek, the river, the endless back and / community, rocks, erosion, buffing, polishing / forth of the sea

22 like windfall letters, / this one's pitted surface / or that one being just the length and width of / my forearm

23 Encircled/ensorcelled fragments / corralled in a temporal / disband pattern / that promises to

24 a different story of migration and waste / the sea does not care what it tosses back at us

25 from a distance, a sleeping seal / remaining organic matter, a lumpy sea scarred tree limb

26 head raised, you see

to rework the image on the page. Michael created a visual broadside and numbered each of the lines to create a sequential reading experience guiding a reader. I also asked him to create a new animation—one that could simulate the movement of driftwood drawn into a whirlpool. Each verse, or phrase, from the poem became its own fragment riding a current of water. Coming and going, the phrases encircled the reader in an ephemeral spiral.

We projected the fourteen-minute piece outdoors on the walls of Seattle's Chophouse Row, juxtaposing the textures of the poem's verses against the rough-hewn siding of the new building. I wanted to evoke the sense of material that had traveled from afar. In the context of a film screening or festival, we realized that the piece would bore audiences in its treatment of time and the extended reading experience. But in this public patio, restaurant goers, residents, and the curious could construct their own meaning through letting poetic fragments float in and out of their imaginations.

Puget Sound Driftwood Circle invited the creative participation of strangers and invented a structure to hold that collaboration. The act of making that work visible was a gesture towards bringing together the collective imagination of the brave writers who'd thought aloud with me—to offer them a work in which they could literally see themselves.

After creating two large-scale projections, I was interested in how movement could be used in a lo-fi, intimate experience. Moving text still operated as the central strategy, but I wanted to make something that an individual would experience only through their active participation rather than "broadcasting" a larger projected work.

Invited to take part in an arts festival at an old Boy Scout camp in West Seattle, I recalled a Nari Baker show at Edmonds Community College in 2012. Baker created View-Master reels with photographs of sites she had traveled to as part of her attempt as a Korean adoptee to reunite with her birth mother. Clicking through the frames of the artist's wordless narrative, I had the sense of turning the pages of a family photo album and peering into a very personal history. Using a View-Master would allow me to explore motion, yet create an interaction for just an individual. It would

Puget Sound Driftwood Circle
▸ Projection at Chophouse Row, Seattle, 2018.

invoke the past, a campground full of kids, but be used to tell an ecological tale of land recently altered.

trout creek ≅ little water explored the history of Longfellow Creek, which flows through Camp Long. To experience and better understand the history of Longfellow Creek, I walked the first several miles of the creek from its origination point in a park through parking lots, playfields, and other built environments until arriving at the place where the creek was daylit. I took detailed notes and passed them along to Tom Stiles, who once again created a sound project with me, indicating where he'd have to look carefully for the posted legacy trail markers directing him to the creek just beyond a public P-patch.

Knowing my designer Michael's appreciation of analog, I called him up and asked if he could design for a View-Master. We discussed taking the poem I wrote about my walk along Longfellow Creek and turning it into a palimpsest—a form that would evoke how the land itself had been written and rewritten. These frames were loaded onto a View-Master and installed inside cabin 4, along with vintage scouting items I borrowed from the Boy Scouts of America office. Under a wooden bunk bed, we placed the audio file recording that captured the sounds and textures of Longfellow Creek. Given the constraints of time and budget for the commission, taking a lo-fi approach was critical to being able to turn around an animated project quickly.

Trout Creek ≅ Little Water

▲ Installation at Camp Long, Seattle, Washington, 2018.

▶ View-Master reel.

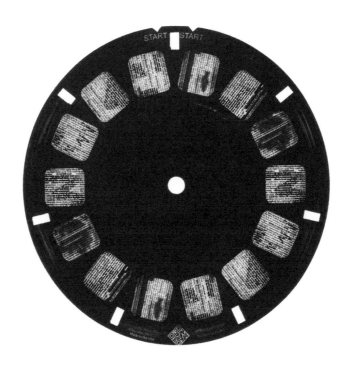

TROUT CREEK
≅
LITTLE WATER

in Roxhill Park, I pull the ribbon
of connection, scout your headwaters

buried long ago beneath storm
drain and sewage pipe,

follow posted trail markers
across asphalt lots emitting heat

past unshaded ball fields to spring
outwards in a thicket of shade,

unburied behind the community gardens,
the turn of water moving over stone—

salmon counted returning to swim
again along the legacy trail,

the tributary at first daylight

As a writer, much of my work involves an intense focus on control—over language and over the page. But to be a writer often means giving up control, through working with publishers and editors. My desire to take greater creative risks grew into thinking with deeper intention about issues of presentation—through bookmaking and performance, but even then, it would take collaboration and working within a community, to help me loosen my need for control. To learn that being open to improvisation and spontaneity is its own form of creativity.

I'm interested in the idea of being "in time" with a poem as it emerges and comes alive. Being in this liminal space before an audience becomes less about performance and more about connection, to one's self and within the context of a larger public or humanity. In this space, I learn about myself as an artist, and I'm afforded the opportunity to truly hear my voice as it echoes back to me.

For many years, I worked at a skyrise in Belltown, a Seattle district just north of downtown once known for low rent and grunge bars, but now gleaming condo towers and construction cranes dominate the landscape. When a neighborhood theater asked if I'd compose a piece for a history cabaret about Belltown, I saw the invitation as an opportunity to better delve into local history.

To spark my writing, the team at the Rendezvous handed me a thick packet of information on local personalities. Pat Suzuki was a Japanese American nightclub singer who had been Seattle's first musician to make it big on Broadway. Pat's narrative, like so many stories of the local Nisei, included the hardships of surviving the internment camps of WWII. Hers was a story worth celebrating and sharing. My question became, "Could I center Pat's story in my own voice?"

For the cabaret, I wrote about Pat Suzuki's connection to Seattle, before her arrival here and after she left it. The piece included imagined fragments of her childhood in Camp Amache, and musings on her decision to leave a successful career on Broadway. The theater assigned me an amazing dramaturg, Sally Ollove, who explained to me how cabaret and musical theater differ. The space of the cabaret is an extension of the artist in real time; the focus becomes the connection between the artist and her audience. There is no need

to inhabit a character, as with musical theater or Broadway. You are exactly who you are. Suzuki was cast in the *Flower Drum Song* as Linda Low, a stripper. Before that, she played a part in the touring *Teahouse of the Autumn Moon* as a minor "Oriental type." Unwilling in the long-term to embrace the limited roles that were available to her as an artist, she chose to return to a less prestigious life that would allow her to perform on her own terms.

This notion of authenticity deeply appealed to me in helping me understand Suzuki's potential motivations for leaving New York, but in also helping me to understand how my delivery of a poem need not be a persona or performance so much as a practice of vulnerability. My earliest models of performed poetry came out of watching Anne Waldman sing/scream "Skin Meat Bones" on stage at Naropa and seeing old footage of Allen Ginsberg sing Blake poems on harmonium while accompanied on guitar by Steven Taylor. This needed to be something different from that.

With the encouragement of the director, I read my piece on stage for the cabaret and performed an a cappella version of "How High the Moon," a song that Suzuki was widely known for singing.

I've always loved the voice. As a teenager, vocal performance was my first passion. But I choked at my audition to music school, and it would take me many years to risk that kind of vulnerability again.

I instead chose to hide behind my poems, distance through object-making, and to choose creative circumstances that allowed me to control what I shared of myself. To the extent that I began to literally remove myself from the work of my animated poems. What I couldn't fully embrace was the value of my own voice. To stand in one's own creative power while being fully seen in her vulnerability is an energetic exchange that gives the artist access to the great ineffable creative source.

CHIBI*

in the vintage footage
Old Blue Eyes calls her
"Patricia" insisting

"You can't get anywhere as a singer
 unless you're Italian."

But Frank, I'm Japanese,
she protested, *I'm from Seattle*

...

at the age of eleven,
little Chiyoko, the all-American girl
sent packing to the High Plains
locked up at Granada War Relocation Center

for the crime of being
descended from the Japanese

...

How does suffering shape a life?

Behind barbed wire,
imprisoned children grew up

to be poet, printmaker, nightclub singer
Lawson [Inada], Arthur [Okamura], Pat [Suzuki]

the record reaching back
so far, we strain to hear the past

*Childhood name for Pat Suzuki, who was the youngest of
four children; translates roughly as "squirt."

in place of cooking or setting
the table, kids play house standing
in imaginary mess-hall lines

                    floating over barbed wire
                    the jade rabbit pounds
                    mochi in the full moon

          over camp, Boy Scouts raise
          the flag, pledging to a country
          that has shunned us

six guard towers armed
with machine guns—here
for our "own safety"

                    Boy's Day: fish streamers
                    fly over barracks, the largest carp
                    to honor an oldest son

          the silk vest handmade for
          a boy's deployment, 1,000 red knots,
          each hand-tied by a different detainee

wheezing from fever
she reshapes the mattress—the canvas
bag stuffed full of hay

                    thin-walled tar paper
                    barracks can't block the biting
                    chill of winter

          before razing the camp
          the last act: building a marker
          for the dead

as "SUZUKI" she "arrived" in Seattle

her ex-husband Norm described
how she sashayed off the street,

decamping from a bit part
at the Moore—where she was cast

as a minor Oriental in
Teahouse of the August Moon

"100 pounds of Nisei dynamite with a voice
that could loosen the tiles on Broadway's towers"

three years later in the role of Linda Low,
the stripper in *Flower Drum Song*,

her signature tune, "I Love Being a Girl,"

we question why a rising star might quit
a bright career in New York theater

preferring Podunk clubs or motherhood
over art—she embraced the person that she always was

to find herself at home in a cabaret
of her own making, that place where

she saw herself reflected in the pale white
faces of the public, where she shattered

stereotype, inhabiting her
skin; flush with more

than anyone from Camp Amache could ever dream

Last summer, I made a piece with my friend the sound artist Steve Peters, which focuses on the voice. Steve persuaded me to visit an ancient barn located in Skagit Valley, just north of Seattle. He planned on making audio recordings of himself "playing" the building and invited me to write and record site-specific texts about the environment of the barn.

In his studio at the Good Shepherd Center, I sat for hours listening as Steve added various sound effects to my vocal tracks to balance my voice with the ambient tones he'd created.

A day before the installation opened to the public, Steve casually asked if I'd like to do an artist's talk together, which evolved into also agreeing to do an improvised short performance. After my anxiety subsided, I picked a handful of my poems that lent themselves to abstraction and space.

Ten minutes before our talk, I watched my friend pull together objects gathered from the property: glass bowls and metallic objects, whatever caught his eye or ear. Objects that he had never played before. After our performance, we talked about how easy it can be to fall back on familiar tropes and gestures that allow one to play it safe while being perceived as improvisatory. The real discovery happens outside of what's known.

Now, the unscripted improvisational is something I pay more attention to as an artist. As much as a poetry reading can be rehearsed or prepared, the poems pre-curated, the stories already laid out, the moment of the performative act can offer up something different, something surprising. No performance has to be the same twice. We learn through the live iteration, choices are made in the present to modify a line, to take a pause. To take in something of our environment and let that vibrate within us for a moment, before we move towards the brightly lit path.

SPLINTERED

door thrown open to fields
of foxglove, allium, bands
of bluebells scoring a field emptied of hops
eyes respond to cloud cover obscuring the sun
this sudden ombré light

baskets swallow a space hollowed
logs round into circular serving
platters, squares of windowpanes,
neatly folded cloths, blankets piled,
napkins stacked that length of seat
that spread of bench

breaking with form

board where the mind
wishes for glass even
in incompletion, the ensō

▲ Splintered

An 8-channel audio installation with sound artist Steve Peters. Site-specific text, hammered into board with recorded sound from manipulated architectural elements and artifacts of the Bitters Co. barn. These recordings were then mixed and recombined with phrases from the poem read aloud. Mount Vernon, Washington, June 2019.

bird droppings coat
whitewashed wooden rafters
a Pollock painting emerging

wooden spoons, glazed
bowls, the oval abdomen
of a spider dancing in air, silken
threads shrouding the shoulders of a vase
candle fingers dissolving with the light

tractor motor moving into
distance, lull of a dozen dead
flies lying atop a berm

seeing cast-type letter forms
fill each frame, I sort
through the printer's drawer

sifting through the leaden heft of language

ENSŌ

Poetry is the highest form of communication that can exist between two individuals. It is, in fact, a form of right speech. Poetry as prayer, invocation, overture, and claim; a fundamental act of defiance through speaking the world into being.

ON COMPLETION

We took our turns at the altar, placing offerings we brought to leave behind. A piece of fabric cherished by her long-deceased mother, handmade drawings, a protective amulet, the widow's gold marriage band. I placed sheets of Chinese grave paper on the second tier of the Mexican ofrenda and wrote my teacher's name, Bill Scheffel, on a blue Post-it note. He left the world through self-immolation on July 8, 2018.

I started writing "Ensō" before my teacher's death and completed it during a long year of grieving and looking inwards.

Once, I believed that I had no ambition. Or, rather, I misunderstood it entirely. I thought that the privilege of the gift is to simply practice, whether or not that work circulates in the world. But there is much wrapped up in the sharing of one's creative and cultural practices, as they can express the best parts of being human, the wisdom we have the opportunity to glean for ourselves and transmit to another.

A gyotaku is a "fish rubbing," the traditional art of making prints from the body of a (dead) fish. As an aside, it's not uncommon to make prints from the placenta of one's newborn. After the shock of going on a squid fishing expedition, it was the idea of the gyotaku that sparked "Ensō." It was the death portrait I needed to compose, about the experience of seeing a life extinguished before my own eyes, to come to terms with what needed to be examined within me to evolve towards a different understanding of devotion.

ENSŌ

an artist inserts ink under skin
shows you how to see

artistry in his craft
what's discerned from studying

claws of a dragon,
finely drawn lines

in the form of waves

appearance of lotus
& cherry blossom in one

flowering gesture
asynchronous

when she sees eye to eye
with the mask of hannya

hanging on a wall, she sees
something she hadn't noticed before—

an expression of sorrow;
reliving one of the few times

her mother reasoned with her

what her parents told her in youth
to make her comply, take down

the poster of the black-haired singer
attired in oversized tee printed with

that same visage, a sad air, gone
by the time her grandfather arrived

for an extended stay; she adapted to
his fear of Japanese ghosts, didn't ask

about the odd look in her eyes, a guise
of wisdom, what marked the image

as the opposite of demonic, *something
to be feared*; her protective potential

in a stranger's office

you dot

the pupil of the daruma,
black
ink
absorbing into the papier-mâché doll,

dilates
to fill   the void

half sighted,

half blind

she trembles in the shadow
of the solar eclipse, the feel

of totality: the temperature on her skin
goes cold by seventeen degrees,

the valley gone silent, an absence
of birdsong around her

fearing she will go blind if
she takes away the protective sheath

she watches sun blotted out,
the soldered seam of light

crackling with the energy of electricity
her hairs standing on end

(a turning of the wheel)

there is no separation between
her and obliteration when she watches

a juvenile squid, *loligo opalescens*,
expire in the weathered palm of

the retired smoke jumper, a marine biologist
presiding over the death scraped

a plastic spoon across its soft body,
activating a rainbow of chromatophores,

ink flooding his grip

an animal died

                    in the making of this poem

cephalopods thrown into a plastic cooler,

       the clear ziplocked bag of bodies

drawn to the Sound

       in the hope of sex

the betrayal of

                a promise   to do no harm

tasting my unfaithfulness

       while wanting to believe the biologist

who said all the right things:

       when asked if the animal sensed pain

       it has a highly developed nervous system

the group of adventurers peppered him

with questions dissecting

       the anatomy of the animal

       holding the creature's gaze

"in its final death throes"

unprepared for the largeness of its eyes

the sight in the distance:

a band of anglers
bouncing fishing poles,

on the pier pulling their catch into
ten-pound buckets in a slow-motion

spray of light
gleaming drips cascading down

a canvas of night

my eyes dazzled by tears

the damp shadow of a squid
smeared across a sheet of Strathmore

the artist admits herself
to the hospital ward where

she contemplates infinity
for forty years:

in the room of the aftermath
of the obliteration of eternity

your heart stops beating
when the lights go black

a moment before, a knock

on the door brings you back
to the present

eyes gradually attuning
to a hundred glimmering lanterns

ascending flight of fire
lanterns at New Year's

the day you leave that life behind—
artwalk revelers drunkenly pull

political prints beneath the warm lights
of a studio practice, a screen inked,

& reinked with an image of a clenched fist—

after twenty years, opening the doors
of creativity for others—you turn away

walk into the icy night where you are
confronted steps away from your former life

with face after face of homeless men, women & children

projected on the side of an edifice
at one of the city's poorest intersections

—portraits by a British photographer

neighbors from the Union Gospel Mission
towering three stories tall—made to look

at what you have feared—renouncing the wage
that could put your family on the street; forsaking

money paid to you for what you gave up
in yourself to be a part of that world,

remembering the margins
to which you always belonged

an ornamental carp leaping into waterfall

on Thanksgiving Day
she seeks out salmon spawning

at Carkeek Park, moving upstream
she finds their silver bodies at rest

in the shallows, in another
part of the creek, a fish

that didn't make it, caught
in a tangle of branches

the plunk of water splashing
as another fights its way forward

a child sees this ceaseless cycle
as an augury of death

No, she says,
they are completing their lives

you take the eclipse inside yourself
the sheet of colored dots decorate

a white room, effacing every shred of
negative space, the colors the spectrum

of light, before an emotion emerges
the place of possibility where lotus

& sakura are born, to bloom together
upheld by your own sense of boundlessness

in the contours of hand-drawn waves
you start to pull your own story

ACKNOWLEDGMENTS

I have felt very fortunate to work with many deeply creative and artful collaborators throughout the years—my thanks to Michael Barakat, Megan Bent, John Cutrone and Seth Thompson, Maura Donegan, William Foley, Scott Keva James, Tomo Nakayama, Sara Parkel, Tom Rorem, Ferenc Suto, and Tai Shan for helping me to take my work in new directions. Thanks also to Rick Benjamin for his sensitive ear.

To Tom Gilroy for his many years of friendship, and to Jim McKay, Patrick So, Michael Stipe, Lisa Gill, Steve Peters, and Shelly Silver for inspiring me to keep going. Thank you Mary Roy for the writing dates.

The Awesome Foundation of Seattle, 4Culture, Jack Straw Cultural Center, the Center for Environmental Art, and the City of Seattle's Office of Arts & Culture all played a critical part in bringing *Heirloom* to fruition. I'm thankful to David Francis and Thendara Kida-Gee for including the project in their curatorial vision, and appreciated the support of the Seattle Parks Department, City Fruit, Don Ricks, Katy Tuttle, and Friends of Piper's Orchard.

Thank you Jessica Rubenacker, Janet Lee, Joshua Heim, Nicole Baker, the Redmond Historical Society, and the Arts Commission of the City of Redmond for opening doors and facilitating my work beyond Seattle.

With infinite gratitude to Tom Stiles for bringing me to see the Yayoi Kusama exhibition.

And with love and appreciation for my fellow adventurers at Atlas Obscura for encouraging a life centered around wonder and curiosity. For inviting me to stand in totality with them during the total eclipse of 2017 in Durkee, Oregon.

Thanks to Bob Leversee for loaning his brain and for helping me to better aim the light from my heart.

This book would not have been possible without the support of my partner, Markus Kortlan Bergman, who taught me to build mountains out of tea dust. I dedicate this book to my ancestors. And to my son, Tomo, for teaching me the value of just being.

CONTENT & IMAGE CREDITS

"Sixteen Pillars" appeared in an earlier form in *Full Bleed: A Journal of Art & Design*, Issue 1.

"Haiku Not Bombs" appeared in an editioned letterpress and offset chapbook of the same name, produced by Booklyn Artists Alliance for its ABC series.

Some of the haiku in this collection were published as the chaplet *Nearly Invisible* from Longhouse Poetry. A small selection of these poems also appeared in the 2013 Festival of Writers Haiku Project produced by Johnny Brewton of X-Ray Book Co. in a limited letterpress edition for the Rensellaerville Library.

The Peter Levitt poem that opens the essay "Mothering Time" is from "A Translation in Winter" from *Within Within* (Black Moss Press, 2008).

Heirloom was first published as "HEIRLOOM: A Piper's Orchard Abecedarian" in *The Goose*: Vol. 14: Issue 1, Article 23. Sections also appeared in *Monarch Review*.

"heyday" was published in *Redmond Reporter*.

Shin Yu Pai's work on this collection was supported by a grant from the City of Seattle's Office of Arts & Culture.

IMAGE CREDITS: Adobe, 2–7; Shin Yu Pai, 8, 12, 19, 118–121, 132; Knox Gardner, 10, 138–9; Art Institute of Chicago / Art Resource, NY, 22; Marc Perlish, 24; Jesse Meredith, 32; Art & Soul Photography, Seattle for object photography found on 41–43, 54, 63-68, 70–73, 115; Noko Pai, 49; John Pomara, 53; Convivio Bookworks, 68; Katy Tuttle, 78–80, 94–109; Michael Barakat, 124, 129-30; James McDaniel, 125; Richard Long. All Rights Reserved, DACS, London / ARS, NY, "Puget Sound Driftwood Circle" Henry Art Gallery, University of Washington, 128; Eric Frommer, 130; fatforehead photography, Pg 133; David Francis, 142, 155; Arzente Fine Arts, 158; Michelle Hagewood, endpaper detail.

BIOGRAPHY

Shin Yu Pai is a poet, essayist, and visual artist. She is the author of several books of poetry, including *AUX ARCS* (La Alameda, 2013), *Adamantine* (White Pine, 2010), *Sightings: Selected Works (2000–2005)* (1913 Press, 2007), and *Equivalence* (La Alameda, 2003).

She served as the fourth poet laureate of the City of Redmond from 2015 to 2017, and has been an artist in residence for the Seattle Art Museum, Town Hall Seattle, and Pacific Science Center. In 2014, she was nominated for a Stranger Genius Award in Literature.

She is a three-time fellow of the MacDowell Colony and has also been in residence at the Ragdale Foundation, Centrum, and the National Park Service. Her visual work has been shown at the Dallas Museum of Art, the McKinney Avenue Contemporary, Three Arts Club of Chicago, and the American Jazz Museum. She lives and works on indigenous land in the traditional territory of Coast Salish peoples, specifically the Duwamish Tribe (Dkhw Duw'Absh), where she produces and curates events centered on curiosity and wonder for Atlas Obscura. For more info, visit www.shinyupai.com.

AUDIO & MULTIMEDIA

To download a recording of Shin Yu Pai reading poems and essays from this book and to hear or see other material related to it, please visit our website, www.entreriosbooks.com/audio. Select this title and enter the password:

DARUMA

Shin Yu Pai recorded at Jack Straw Cultural Center
Seattle, Washington

September 24, 2019
Recording Engineer: Daniel Guenther

SHIN YU PAI

UNCOLLECTED HAIKU
2005-2019

retiring the half-blind
daruma to desk drawer—
a dream deferred

in the flagship office
an abandoned cardboard box
marked *basura*

row of SWAT team cops
swarm the flat—posted signage:
"training in progress"

the singer's handheld
daf dances in her grasp
metal bangles jangling

grenadine glass vase
gems in a polished colander
gleam like arils

plastic flowers
adorning the roadside
descanso—evergreen

brushing grave
paper ash from
a black sweater

opening one eye
in a lake of ghee, deep
in the primordial soup

talking to a friend about
a film on Milarepa, I describe it
as "slow"

first day, panchakarma
one woman can't stop talking
about coffee & toast

loving the guru
despising the guru & liking
him somewhat again

scrubbing lipstick off
a yogi's tea mug at the Marin
County retreat

Father's Day: men in
yellow & pink polo shirts
play bocce on the green

these invisible
braces make my mouth sweat like
foot-binding for the teeth

sheep outside my cottage
plump up, in the mirror my figure
grows rounder

nearly invisible:
the carrot yellow lotion
splattered on mustard walls

after escorting the giant
spider back outside, bolting
the kitchen door

that angry fly just
gets angrier, can't sense
the door just opened

Kansas billboard "fill
in the gap" dental—the class
gulf, the tooth void

outside Mrs. Baird's
man scatters hunks of bread
no birds for miles

herds of cows huddled
in shade beneath a billboard ad
of the golden arches

roadside, daybreak—
the fleet of parked semis stir
from fog like slow heifers

"COMING FALL 09"
Concho Commons Spring 2010:
still an overgrown lot

pondering how
the leaves of that plastic plant
broke free to the floor

passing through Hot Springs
I spy the sign "Woo Pig Sooie"
picture Chinese BBQ

bullet holes riddling
the posted speed limit—
central Arkansas

end the war now
flyers from last year's rally
plastered beneath the underpass

wandering through fields
of brightly colored gourds spotted
with decay, I think of Yayoi

winter at Green Lake:
spandexed runners replaced with
cross-country skiers

back from Montreal
to snow & tent city morphed
back to car park

old ladies talking
about the recession at
the local thrift shop

berry foragers
at Green Lake: in the back alley
a man picks thru trash

that man in my life
that rock in my shoe
to be thrown away

Occupy Ikea:
lonely heart meet-ups
over unlimited joe

runaway roll of gauze
left behind at the stabbing
scene yellow police tape

returning childbirthing
books to the library after
the blighted ovum

after the fight, seeing
him stare out the window as if
waiting for me to come home

quarreling w/ the Latina
lunch lady about her version
of bi bim bap, pobre teriyaki

vowing to get glasses when
the Copland quote outside symphony
hall grows obscure

swishing the toilets,
cleaning the house, I ready
the mind to write

dusting slatted metal
heat vents with a Q-tip,
I sound out a tune

the scarlet bouquet of
"everlasting love" fading
at the tulip fest

someone's spouse passes out
while the women watch slides
of birth by C-section

just shy of thirty-five
weeks, tsukimi chakai—I gaze
at the ripening moon

watching the cop don
a blue latex glove before
prodding the man passed out

busing over
Ballard Bridge anxious of
when the "big one" hits

students stand up for
freedom, occupy the legislative yuan,
dear motherland, never give up

far eastern sweet
potatoes, the dark
outline of Taiwan

at the eye exam
wondering all of the sudden where
faking it gets me

ferry boats crossing
the Sound, dots disappearing
like swimmers

thinking today of Stevens—
thirteen ways of viewing
a construction crane

trying to recall the word
for "gaslighting" my brain
pulls up "waterboarding"

hundreds of students
drowned when the ship went down
all just kids

arguing about the room
temp, I snap at my husband
to "take off his pants"

husband snoring,
the baby saws logs, I lie awake
stomach growling

on the road to Tiger's Nest
mistaking birdcalls from Chinese tourists
for cries of pain

ascending the dusty path
my companion: the sharpened
walking stick

winded from altitude
knowing yet I will not
die I will not die

gather a group of strangers
together to raise a strand of prayer flags
and make an auspicious day

advised to arm myself
with a rock to guard against wild dogs
I discard the stone in a ditch

rice grains in the window
seat at the temple
remnants of offerings

the city paid
leaf blower aims his wand at
the tent encampment

seeing a fiddlehead fern for
the first time my boy draws
his hand into a curl

yellowed maple leaves
gleaming on black asphalt
Seattle's forgotten dead

confusing leaf fall for
public remembrance, memorials
on every corner